Earning and Spending in Rural India: The Case of Tamil Nadu

E. Karthikeya

Earning and Spending in Rural India: The Case of Tamil Nadu

E. Karthikeya

Academica Press
Washington~London

Library of Congress Cataloging-in-Publication Data

Names: Karthikeya, E. (author)
Title: Earning and spending in rural india : the case of tamil nadu | Karthikeya, E.
Description: Washington : Academica Press, 2022. | Includes references.
Identifiers: LCCN 2022952202 | ISBN 9781680536829 (hardcover) | 9781680536836 (e-book)

Contents

Chapter I 1

Chapter II
Review of Literature 19

Chapter III
Tribal Development 41

Chapter IV
Profile of The Study Area 59

Chapter V
Differences Between the Households Living BPL and APL 67

Chapter VI
Conclusion 81

Bibliography 99

Maps 107

Study Area Photographs 111

Charts 113

Chapter I

1.1 Introduction

India is the second largest country in terms of population; and, first largest country in terms of people living below poverty line (BPL). India's GDP (Gross Domestic Product) is growing at faster rate as compared to many countries in the world (vide Table 1.1). But the population living in slums (vide Table 1.2), sleeping and defecating on the roadsides (vide Table 1.5) and begging is also increasing. Number of world class riches in India is increasing (vide Table 1.3 and 1.4); but poverty levels have not decreased. The levels of poverty and incidence of poverty are higher in rural areas and among Scheduled Caste (SC) and Scheduled Tribe (ST) populations. Hence the present study has made an attempt to understand the issues relating to poverty in a tribal village namely Puliyur located in Jawadhu Hills in Thiruvannamalai district, Tamil Nadu.

1.2 Scheduled Tribes (STs)

Largest tribal population is found in Africa. Most of the tribal population lives in remote forest and hill regions. Government of India has notified 75 tribal communities. According to 2011 census, the ST population in India was around 10 crores accounting for around nine per cent of the India's total population (vide Table 6). Of them, 90 per cent are living in rural areas and the remaining 10 per cent are living in urban areas. More than half of ST population is concentrated in Central India namely Madhya Pradesh (14.69%), Chhattisgarh (7.5%), Jharkhand (8.29%), Andhra Pradesh (5.7%), Maharashtra (10.08%), Orissa (9.2%), Gujarat (8.55%) and Rajasthan (8.86%). The other distinct area is the North East (Assam, Nagaland, Mizoram, Manipur, Meghalaya, Tripura, Sikkim and Arunachal Pradesh). The statistically strong scheduled tribe groups include Santhal, Gond, Bhil, Oraon. Smaller tribal groups are to be found in A&N Islands (Andamanese, Onges), Kerala and Tamil Nadu (Paniyans and Kattunaickens).

Imperial Gazetteer of India, 1911, defined a tribe as a "Collection of families bearing a common name, speaking a common dialect, occupying or professing to occupy a common territory and is not usually endogamous though originally might have been so."

1.3 Tribal Sex Ratio

Sex ratio in respect of STs is 990 which is higher than national average of 943. Also, ST sex ratio has improved from 978 females per 1000 males in 2001 to 990 in 2011. Goa, Kerala, Arunachal Pradesh, Odisha, Chhattisgarh, etc., have shown high ST sex ratio while Jammu & Kashmir has shown the lowest ST sex ratio at 924 in 2011.

1.4 Tribal Literacy Rate

The tribal literacy rate increased from 8.53 per cent in 1961 to 58.96 percent in 2011. The total population literacy rate increased from 28.30 per cent in 1961 to 72.99 per cent in 2011.

1.5 Tribal Poverty in India

The Planning Commission in India has estimated the poverty ratios on the basis of Tendulkar Methodology. As per these estimates, in 2011-12, 45 per cent of ST in rural areas and 24 per cent of ST in urban areas lived BPL. These estimates for non-ST population were 26 per cent and 14 per cent respectively (vide Table 7).

1.6 Tribal Population in Tamil Nadu

Total population of Tamil Nadu is 7. 12 crores as per 2011 census; the tribal population is 7.9 lakhs. The tribal population in the State has raised from 1.04 per cent of the total population in 2001 to 1.8 per cent of the total population in 2011(vide Table 8).

1.7 Tribal Groups in Tamil Nadu

There are 36 different tribes, present in almost all the districts, across 2,860 villages located in 63 blocks of the state (vide Table 9). They are predominantly in rural areas, and of these, around 5 lakh live in 13 districts, namely, Krishnagiri, Dharmapuri, Vellore, Tiruvannamalai, Salem, Villupuram, Erode, Namakkal, Coimbatore, The Nilgiris, Dindigul, Trichy and Kanniyakumari. The remaining 1.5 lakh (20%) population live in urban areas. The Nilgiris district has the highest percentage of STs (4.5%), followed by Dharmapuri district (4.2%) (TNRTP, 2017).

1.8 Statement of the problem

Though many tribal development programmes have been implemented in India and Tamil Nadu, a substantial population of STs live BPL, while a small proportion of STs live above poverty line (APL). Hence naturally there arise some questions: why some people continue to live BPL for a long period? How some people could manage to go APL? What are the differences between these two groups namely STs APL & STs BPL? How do they differ? Where do they differ? Why do they differ? Can the STs BPL come APL?

1.9 Objective of the Study

To understand the differences between the STs living BPL and STs living APL.

1.10 Hypothesis of the Study

There is no difference between the STs living BPL and the STs living APL.

1.11 Methodology

1.11.1 Selection of the Study Context

To understand the difference between the STs living BPL and the STs living APL, a region with ST population has been chosen. That is Jawadhu Hills, located in Eastern Ghats in Tamil Nadu (Thiruvannamalai District). In this region a village called Puliyur has been chosen purposively. There are 419 households.

1.11.2 Sampling

Out of the households mentioned above, a sample of 113 households have been chosen randomly.

Beside the primary data collected from the sample households, secondary data have been used to locate study village and to describe the profile of the study region.

1.11.3 Conceptualization of Poverty

After collecting the primary data, the sample households have been grouped into two categories on the basis of the per capita income at household level. The two categories are

1. The households BPL and 2. The households APL.

The per capita annual income limit decided to categorize the households is Rs. 18,250, which is equivalent to Rs. 50 per day per person. As per this working definition of poverty there are 76 households BPL and 37 households APL.

All the relevant details have been compared for these two gropes of households for understanding the reason for poverty.

1.12 Scope of the Study

Understanding the differences between the households BPL and APL would help to design proper polices to alleviate poverty among the STs.

1.13 Limitation of the Study

The study depends on the data collected during the year 2015 - 2016. This particular year would have been different in terms of income and expenditure for different households. Relative position of the households may be different in different years. However, this study could not capture those differences.

1.14 Organization of the Thesis

This thesis has six chapters. First Chapter discusses the background of the study, while the second Chapter presents a brief survey of related literature. The Third Chapter deals with tribal development programmes through the Five Year Plans. Fourth Chapter deals with profile of the research area. The Fifth Chapter deals with analysis and interpretation of data. The last Chapter is set for presenting a brief summary of conclusion, findings and recommendations of the present study.

Table 1.1 India's Gross domestic products (GDP) in 1980 -2017 (in Rs.)

Year	Gross Domestic Product at constant prices	Year	Gross Domestic Product at constant prices
1980	5.3	2002	3.9
1981	6.0	2003	7.9
1982	3.5	2004	7.8
1983	7.3	2005	9.3
1984	3.8	2006	9.3
1985	5.3	2007	9.8
1986	4.8	2008	3.9
1987	4.0	2009	8.5
1988	9.6	2010	10.3
1989	5.9	2011	6.6
1990	5.5	2012	5.1
1991	1.1	2013	6.9
1992	5.5	2014	7.2
1993	4.8	2015	8.0 (est.)
1994	6.7	2016	7.1 (est.)
1995	7.6	2017	6.7 (est.)
1996	7.6	2002	3.9
1997	4.1	2003	7.9
1998	6.2	2004	7.8
1999	8.5	2005	9.3
2000	4.0	2006	9.3
2001	4.9	2007	9.8

Source: https://www.indexmundi.com/india/gdp_real_growth_rate.html (Accessed in 22-11-2018)

Table 1.2 Slum Population - Census 2011

S. No.	State	Slum Population	SC	ST	Total Slum population (%)
	India	**65,494,604**	**13,354,080**	**2,216,533**	**5.41**
1	Maharashtra	11,848,423	1,863,882	364,254	10.54
2	Andhra Pradesh	10,186,934	1,428,212	270,556	12.04
3	Tamil Nadu	**5,798,459**	**1,853,315**	**30,996**	**8.04**
4	West Bengal	6,418,594	1,060,811	106,373	7.03
5	Madhya Pradesh	5,688,993	1,251,713	356,481	7.83
6	Uttar Pradesh	6,239,965	1,373,211	19,186	3.12
7	Karnataka	3,291,434	922,589	172,129	5.39
8	Chhattisgarh	1,898,931	338,098	174,050	7.43
9	Rajasthan	2,068,000	582,562	100,675	3.02
10	Delhi	1,785,390	482,870	0	10.63
11	Orissa	1,560,303	321,167	199,836	3.72
12	Gujarat	1,680,095	186,577	125,538	2.78
13	Haryana	1,662,305	497,042	0	6.56
14	Punjab	1,460,518	581,984	0	5.26
15	Bihar	1,237,682	260,442	16,630	1.19
16	Jammu and Kashmir	662,062	11,136	10,797	5.28
17	Uttarakhand	487,741	91,953	2,321	4.84
18	Jharkhand	372,999	58,164	66,680	1.13
19	Kerala	202,048	21,923	411	0.60
20	Assam	197,266	42,358	3,702	0.63
21	Puducherry	144,573	34,521	0	11.58
22	Tripura	139,780	40,291	3,337	3.80
23	Chandigarh	95,135	29,230	0	9.01
24	Nagaland	82,324	0	64,253	4.16
25	Mizoram	78,561	69	73,552	7.16
26	Himachal Pradesh	61,312	16,062	488	0.89
27	Meghalaya	57,418	1,589	40,752	1.94
28	Sikkim	31,378	1,658	8,745	5.14
29	Goa	26,247	651	112	1.80
30	Arunachal Pradesh	15,562	0	4,631	1.12
31	Andaman and Nicobar Islands	14,172	0	48	3.72

Source: https://www.census2011.co.in/slums.php (Accessed 22-11-2018)

Table 1.3 Continent-wise Billionaires

World rank	Continent	Number of billionaires	Richest in the continent	Net worth in billions (USD)
–	World	2,208	Jeff Bezos	132.8
1	Asia	719	Ma Huateng	51.1
2	North America	631	Jeff Bezos	132.8
3	Europe	559	Bernard Arnault	83.7
4	South America	85	Jorge Paulo Lemann	29.7
5	Oceania	35	Gina Rinehart	17.40
6	Africa	25	Aliko Dangote	14.1

Source: https://en.wikipedia.org/wiki/List_of_countries_by_the_number_of_billionaires (Accessed 22-11-2018)

Table 1.4 Top 50 Billionaires in India

<table>
<tr><th>India</th><th>World Rank</th><th>Name</th><th>Age</th><th>City of residence</th><th>Net Worth in US$ (billion)</th></tr>
<tr><td>1</td><td>19</td><td>Mukesh Ambani</td><td>61</td><td>Mumbai</td><td>40.1</td></tr>
<tr><td>2</td><td>58</td><td>Azim Premji</td><td>73</td><td>Bangalore</td><td>18.8</td></tr>
<tr><td>3</td><td>62</td><td>Lakshmi Mittal</td><td>68</td><td>London</td><td>18.5</td></tr>
<tr><td>4</td><td>98</td><td>Shiv Nadar</td><td>73</td><td>New Delhi</td><td>14.6</td></tr>
<tr><td>5</td><td>115</td><td>Dilip Shanghvi</td><td>63</td><td rowspan="4">Mumbai</td><td>12.8</td></tr>
<tr><td>6</td><td>127</td><td>Kumar Birla</td><td>51</td><td>11.8</td></tr>
<tr><td>7</td><td>143</td><td>Uday Kotak</td><td>59</td><td>10.7</td></tr>
<tr><td>8</td><td>151</td><td>Radhakishan Damani</td><td>63</td><td>10</td></tr>
<tr><td>9</td><td>154</td><td>Gautam Adani</td><td>56</td><td>Ahmedabad</td><td>9.7</td></tr>
<tr><td>10</td><td>170</td><td>Cyrus Poonawalla</td><td>73</td><td>Mumbai</td><td>9.1</td></tr>
<tr><td>11</td><td rowspan="2">176</td><td>Savitri Jindal</td><td>68</td><td>Hisar</td><td>8.8</td></tr>
<tr><td>12</td><td>Sunil Mittal</td><td>61</td><td rowspan="2">New Delhi</td><td>8.8</td></tr>
<tr><td>13</td><td>265</td><td>Kushal Pal Singh</td><td>87</td><td>6.4</td></tr>
<tr><td>14</td><td rowspan="2">274</td><td>Acharya Balkrishna</td><td>46</td><td>Uttarakhand</td><td>6.3</td></tr>
<tr><td>15</td><td>Vikram Lal</td><td>76</td><td>New Delhi</td><td>6.3</td></tr>
<tr><td>16</td><td>281</td><td>Nusli Wadia</td><td>74</td><td>Mumbai</td><td>6.2</td></tr>
<tr><td>17</td><td>289</td><td>Benu Gopal Bangur</td><td>87</td><td>Kolkata</td><td>6</td></tr>
<tr><td>18</td><td>372</td><td>Kalanithi Maran</td><td>53</td><td>Chennai</td><td>5.2</td></tr>
<tr><td>19</td><td rowspan="3">388</td><td>Subhash Chandra</td><td>67</td><td>Mumbai</td><td>5</td></tr>
<tr><td>20</td><td>Pankaj Patel</td><td>67</td><td>Ahmedabad</td><td>5</td></tr>
<tr><td>21</td><td>M. A. Yousuf Ali</td><td>63</td><td>Abu dhabi</td><td>5</td></tr>
</table>

India	World Rank	Name	Age	City of residence	Net Worth in US$ (billion)
22	404	Ajay Piramal	63		4.9
23	422	Bajaj Brothers		Mumbai	4.8
24	466	Rahul & Kapil Bhatia	-	New Delhi	4.5
25	480	Micky Jagtiani	66	Dubai	4.4
26	499	Rahul Bajaj	80	Pune	4.3
27	527	Pawan Munjal	67	Delhi	4.1
28	550	B. R. Shetty	76	Abu Dhabi	4.1
29	572	Sudhir & Samir Mehta	-	Ahmedabad	3.9
30		B. Ravi Pillai	65	Dubai	3.9
31	606	Mangal Prabhat Lodha	62	Mumbai	3.7
32	629	Kiran Mazumdar-Shaw	65	Bangalore	3.6
33		Karsanbhai Patel	74	Ahmedabad	3.6
34	652	Gurbachan & Kuldip Singh Dhingra	-	New Delhi	3.5
35		Baba Kalyani	69	Pune	3.5
36	679	Shashi & Ravi Ruia	-	Mumbai	3.4
37	703	Anil Agarwal	64	London	3.3
38		Ashwin Dani	75		3.3
39	729	Sameer Gehlaut	44	Mumbai	3.2
40	766	Rajan Raheja	64		3.1
41		Hasmukh Chudgar	84	Ahmedabad	3
42	791	Rakesh Jhunjhunwala	58	Mumbai	3
43		Smita Crishna-Godrej	67		2.9
44	822	Adi Godrej	76		2.9
45		Jamshyd Godrej	69	Mumbai	2.9
46		Nadir Godrej	67		2.9
47		Rishad Naoroji	67		2.9
48		Aloke Lohia	59	Bangkok	2.8
49	859	Chandru Raheja	75		2.8
50	688	Anil Ambani	59	Mumbai	2.7

Source: https://en.wikipedia.org/wiki/Forbes_list_of_Indian_billionaires (Accessed 22-11-2018)

Table 1.5 The percentage of people go for open defecation and rank

Rank	Country	Value
1	Eritrea	76.03
2	Niger	71.31
3	Chad	67.59
4	Benin	55.16
5	Togo	50.68
6	Namibia	49.88
7	São Tomé and Principe	49.79
8	Burkina Faso	47.98
9	Madagascar	43.93
10	Liberia	42.26
11	Solomon Islands	41.05
12	Cambodia	40.57
13	**India**	**39.84**
14	Somalia	39.10
15	Mozambique	35.99
16	Kiribati	34.65
17	Angola	32.84
18	Mauritania	30.11
19	Lesotho	30.04
20	Nepal	29.83
21	Cabo Verde	28.08
22	Ethiopia	27.16
23	Sudan	26.67
24	Zimbabwe	26.49
25	Nigeria	25.54
26	Central African Republic	23.92
27	Côte d'Ivoire	23.66
28	Timor-Leste	23.61
29	Djibouti	22.83
30	Lao PDR	22.07
31	Yemen	19.98
32	Haiti	19.03
33	Sierra Leone	18.81
34	Ghana	18.75
35	Botswana	16.86
36	Guinea-Bissau	16.06
37	Guinea	15.36
38	Zambia	15.19

Rank	Country	Value
39	Senegal	15.11
40	Bolivia	14.49
41	Afghanistan	13.55
42	Papua New Guinea	12.91
43	Indonesia	12.45
44	Dem. Rep. Congo	12.08
45	Kenya	12.03
46	Pakistan	11.55
47	Tanzania	11.26
48	Swaziland	10.94
49	Mongolia	9.66
50	Mali	8.05
51	Congo	8.04
52	Morocco	7.58
53	Peru	7.28
54	Honduras	7.22
55	Tuvalu	7.09
56	Cameroon	7.08
57	Nicaragua	6.97
58	Malawi	6.47
59	Suriname	6.32
60	Uganda	6.21
61	Philippines	5.74
62	Guatemala	5.60
63	Venezuela	4.86
64	Myanmar	4.67
65	Equatorial Guinea	4.42
66	Colombia	3.94
67	Vietnam	3.85
68	Dominica	3.75
69	Grenada	3.54
70	Panama	3.39
71	St. Vincent and the Grenadines	3.36
72	Dominican Republic	3.29
73	Burundi	3.14
74	Gabon	3.03
75	Ecuador	3.00
76	Sri Lanka	2.65
77	Brunei	2.60
78	Nauru	2.59
79	South Africa	2.25
80	Rwanda	2.12

Rank	Country	Value
81	Brazil	1.98
82	Mexico	1.68
83	Vanuatu	1.68
84	El Salvador	1.56
85	China	1.51
86	Argentina	1.35
87	Belize	1.23
88	Tunisia	0.89
89	Barbados	0.83
90	Syrian Arab Republic	0.81
91	Algeria	0.80
92	St. Lucia	0.79
93	Jamaica	0.74
94	Macedonia	0.69
95	Guyana	0.63
96	The Gambia	0.61
97	Comoros	0.59
98	Uruguay	0.54
99	Iran	0.54
100	St. Kitts and Nevis	0.44
101	Paraguay	0.38
102	Cuba	0.36
103	Malaysia	0.35
104	Turkey	0.33
105	Thailand	0.27
106	Antigua and Barbuda	0.26
107	Trinidad and Tobago	0.26
108	Albania	0.20
109	Costa Rica	0.19
110	Croatia	0.19
111	Azerbaijan	0.16
112	Mauritius	0.14
113	Fiji	0.14
114	Moldova	0.13
115	Samoa	0.13
116	Chile	0.11
117	Bangladesh	0.11
118	Serbia	0.07
119	Egypt	0.07
120	Tajikistan	0.07
121	Montenegro	0.06
122	Turkmenistan	0.05

Rank	Country	Value
123	Lebanon	0.04
124	Iraq	0.02
125	Jordan	0.01
126	Kazakhstan	0.01
127	Ukraine	0.00
128	New Caledonia	0.00
128	Dem. People's Rep. Korea	0.00
128	Palau	0.00
128	Greece	0.00
128	Bulgaria	0.00
128	Belgium	0.00
128	Armenia	0.00
128	Tonga	0.00
128	Georgia	0.00
128	New Zealand	0.00
128	Poland	0.00
128	Saudi Arabia	0.00
128	Germany	0.00
128	Greenland	0.00
128	Netherlands	0.00
128	Norway	0.00
128	Oman	0.00
128	Portugal	0.00
128	Libya	0.00
128	Luxembourg	0.00
128	Malta	0.00
128	Belarus	0.00
128	Austria	0.00
128	Cayman Islands	0.00
128	Lithuania	0.00
128	Puerto Rico	0.00
128	Qatar	0.00
128	Singapore	0.00
128	Latvia	0.00
128	Sweden	0.00
128	Uzbekistan	0.00
128	Australia	0.00
128	The Bahamas	0.00
128	France	0.00
128	Ireland	0.00
128	Iceland	0.00
128	Bhutan	0.00

Rank	Country	Value
128	Estonia	0.00
128	Korea	0.00
128	Kuwait	0.00
128	Russia	0.00
128	Finland	0.00
128	United Kingdom	0.00
128	Canada	0.00
128	Cyprus	0.00
128	San Marino	0.00
128	United Arab Emirates	0.00
128	Bahrain	0.00
128	Czech Republic	0.00
128	Liechtenstein	0.00
128	Andorra	0.00
128	Monaco	0.00
128	Israel	0.00
128	Italy	0.00
128	Spain	0.00
128	Japan	0.00
128	Romania	0.00
128	Seychelles	0.00
128	Denmark	0.00
128	Hungary	0.00
128	United States	0.00
128	Slovak Republic	0.00
128	Slovenia	0.00
128	Bosnia and Herzegovina	0.00
128	Switzerland	0.00
128	Hong Kong SAR, China	0.00
128	Kyrgyz Republic	0.00

Source: https://www.indexmundi.com/facts/indicators/SH.STA.ODFC.ZS/rankings (Accessed 22-11-2018) Note: 2015 ranking in world-wide.

Table 1.6 State-wise overall and ST population. (Percentage)

S. No	States	Total population (in 00,000)	ST Population	% of ST population
1	Andhra Pradesh	493.0	26.3	5.3
2	Arunachal Pradesh	13.0	9.5	68.8
3	Assam	312.0	38.8	12.4
4	Bihar	104.0	13.3	1.3
5	Chhattisgarh	255.4	78.2	30.6
6	Goa	4.5	1.4	10.2
7	Gujarat	604.3	89.1	14.8
8	Haryana	253.5	NST	NA
9	Himachal Pradesh	68.6	3.9	5.7
10	J&K	125.4	14.9	11.9
11	Jharkhand	329.8	86.4	26.2
12	Karnataka	610.9	42.4	7.0
13	Kerala	334.0	4.8	1.5
14	Madhya Pradesh	726.2	153.14	21.1
15	Maharashtra	112.3	105.1	9.4
16	Manipur	28.5	11.6	40.9
17	Meghalaya	29.6	25.5	86.1
18	Mizoram	10.9	10.3	94.4
19	Nagaland	19.7	17.1	86.5
20	Orissa	419.7	95.9	22.8
21	Punjab	277.4	NST	NA
22	Rajasthan	685.4	92.3	13.5
23	Sikkim	6.1	2.0	33.8
24	Tamil Nadu	721.4	7.9	1.1
25	Telangana	119.7	920.5	7.7
26	Tripura	36.7	11.6	31.8
27	Uttarakhand	100.8	2.9	2.9
28	Uttar Pradesh	199.8	11.3	0.6
29	West Bengal	912.7	52.9	5.8
30	A & N Islands	3.8	0.2	7.5
31	Chandigarh	10.5	NST	NA
32	D & N Haveli	3.4	1.7	52.0
33	Daman & Diu.	2.4	0.1	6.3

S. No	States	Total population (in 00,000)	ST Population	% of ST population
34	Delhi	167.8	NST	NA
35	Lakshadweep	0.64	0.6	94.8
36	Puducherry	12.4	NST	NA
	All India	1210.8	1045.4	8.6

Source: Census 2011, Office of the Registrar General, India.
NST: No notified Scheduled Tribes, NA: Not Available.

Table 1.7 State-wise STs Poverty Ratio of ST Population (Percentage)

Si. No	States	Scheduled Tribes				Non-Scheduled Tribes			
		1993-94	2004-05	2009-10	2011-12	1993-94	2004-05	2009-10	2011-12
1	Andhra Pradesh	58.4	60.3	40.2	24.1	48.3	32.3	22.7	11.0
2	Assam	55.6	28.8	32.0	33.4	55.3	36.4	39.9	33.9
3	Bihar	73.3	59.3	64.4	59.3	62.5	55.7	55.3	34.4
4	Chhattisgarh	66.1	65.5	66.8	52.6	56.0	55.1	56.1	44.6
5	Delhi	0	0	0	0	16.2	15.6	7.6	12.9
6	Gujarat	53.2	57.1	48.6	36.5	43.3	39.1	26.6	21.5
7	Haryana	69.7	0.0	49.6	3.3	40.2	24.8	18.6	11.6
8	Himachal Pradesh	62.4	35.4	22.0	9.5	36.9	25.0	9.1	8.5
9	Jammu & Kashmir	74.5	26.5	3.1	16.3	32.4	14.1	8.1	11.5
10	Jharkhand	72.6	60.6	51.0	51.6	65.9	51.6	41.4	40.8
11	Karnataka	71.2	50.5	21.3	30.8	56.8	37.5	26.1	24.5
12	Kerala	40.9	56.9	24.4	41.0	34.0	20.2	12.0	9.2
13	Madhya Pradesh	70.2	80.0	61.9	53.3	49.1	53.6	42.0	35.0
14	Maharashtra	74.2	73.2	51.7	61.6	59.3	47.9	29.5	24.7
15	Orissa	82.2	84.4	66.0	63.5	63.2	60.8	39.2	35.7
16	Punjab	35.9	30.7	16.1	0	20.4	22.1	14.6	7.7
17	Rajasthan	64.1	59.3	35.9	41.4	40.9	35.8	26.4	16.1
18	Tamil Nadu	57.0	47.3	11.5	36.8	51.2	37.5	21.2	15.8
19	Uttar Pradesh	49.6	42.0	49.8	27.0	51.0	42.7	39.3	30.4
20	Uttarakhand	54.9	32.4	20.0	11.9	37.0	35.1	13.7	11.7
21	West Bengal	66.7	54.3	32.9	50.1	42.6	38.2	28.8	22.5
	All India	65.9	62.3	47.4	45.3	50.3	41.8	33.3	25.4

Source: Statistical Profile of Scheduled Tribes in India 2013.

Table 1.8 Tamil Nadu Tribal Population by District

Si.No	District	Total population (in 00000)	ST population (in 000)	Percentage
1	Chennai	46.4	10.0	0.21
2	Kancheepuram	39.9	41.2	1.03
3	Thiruvallur	37.2	47.2	1.26
4	Cuddalor	26.0	15.7	0.60
5	Villupuram	34.5	74.8	2.16
6	Vellore	39.3	72.9	1.85
7	**Thiruvannamalai**	**24.6**	**90.9**	**3.69**
8	Salem	34.8	119.3	3.42
9	Namakkal	17.2	57.0	3.30
10	Dharmapuri	15.0	63.0	4.18
11	Krishnagiri	18.7	22.3	1.19
12	Erode	22.5	21.8	0.97
13	Coimbatore	34.5	28.3	0.81
14	Tiruppur	24.7	5.4	0.22
15	The Nilgiris	7.3	32.8	4.46
16	Tiruchirappalli	27.2	18.1	0.66
17	Karur	10.6	0.5	0.05
18	Perabalur	5.6	2.5	0.45
19	Ariyalur	7.5	10.7	1.42
20	Thanjavur	24.0	3.5	0.14
21	Nagapattinam	16.1	3.7	0.23
22	Thiruvarur	12.6	3.0	0.23
23	Pudukkottai	16.1	1.2	0.07
24	Madurai	30.3	11.0	0.36
25	Theni	12.4	1.8	0.14
26	Dindigul	21.5	8.0	0.64
27	Ramanathapuram	13.5	1.1	0.08
28	Viruthunagar	19.4	2.2	0.11
29	Sivaganga	13.3	0.7	0.05
30	Tirunelveli	30.7	10.2	0.33
31	Thoothukkudi	17.5	4.9	0.28
32	Kanniyakumari	18.7	7.2	0.38
	Tamil Nadu	721.4	79.4	1.10

Sources: Census of India 2011.

Table 1.9 List of Tribal Community in Tamil Nadu (listed by Government of India)

1.Adiyan	21. Malai Pandaram
2. Aranadan	22. Malai Vedan
3. Eravallan	23. Malakkuravan
4. Irular	24. Malasar
5. Kadar	25. Malayali (in Dharmapuri, North Arcot, Pudukottai, Salem, South Arcot and Tiruchirapali districts)
6. Kammara (excluding Kanyakumari district and Shenkottah taluk of Tirunelveli district)	26. Malayekandi
7. Kanikaran, Kanikkar (in Kanyakumari district and Shenkottah and Ambasamudram taluks of Tirunelveli district)	27. Mannan
8. Kaniyan, Kanyan	28. Mudugar, Muduvan
9. Kattunayakan	29. Muthuvan
10. Kochu Velan	30. Palleyan
11. Konda Kapus	31. Palliyan
12. Kondareddis	32. Palliyar
13. Koraga	33. Paniyan
14. Kota (excluding Kanyakumari district and Shenkottah taluk of Tirunelveli district)	34. Sholaga
15. Kudiya, Melakudi	35. Toda (excluding Kanyakumari district and Shenkottah Taluk of Tirunelveli district)
16. Kurichchan	36. Uraly
17. Kurumbas (in the Nilgiris district)	
18. Kurumans	
19. Maha Malasar	
20. Malai Arayan	

Source: Statistical Profile of Scheduled Tribes in India 2013.

References:

Government of India (2011): Census Office of the Registrar General, Government of India.

Government of Tamil Nadu (2017): "Tamil Nadu Rural Transformation Project (TNRTP)," Report.

Ministry of Tribal Affairs (2013): Statistical Profile of Scheduled Tribes in India, Government of India.

Chapter II

Review of Literature

2.1 Introduction

The poverty issues have been diseased by economists for long. Also, poverty is not new to the world. Miserable living condition have been experienced by people for long not only in developing countries but also in developed countries including Europe. Adam Smith wrote a book on "Wealth of the Nations," Gunnar Myedal wrote a book on "Poverty of Nations," which is popularly known as "Asian Drama." In India poverty literature started with the book entitled "Poverty in India" by N Rath and V. M. Dandekar. There was a long discussion on the determinants and measurement of poverty level and incidence of poverty. Calorie intake, monthly per capita consumption expenditure (MPCE), per capita income etc. have been used to determine the existence of poverty. Different kinds of methodologies have also been designed. However, there is no significant impact on poverty reduction.

It was believed that the people spend more on consumption would have better health. It was on this basis only MPCE was used to identify poverty. However in recent years, thanks to the efforts taken by governments, particularly Government of Tamil Nadu, liquor sales have been promoted. The liquor availability has been improved. As a result the liquor consumption and consumption expenditure have increased. It, however, does not mean that the increased consumption expenditure has improved the health status of the people. Therefore, under the present condition, consumption expenditure cannot be considered as the index of poverty. Therefore other indicators need to be considered for defining poverty.

Living condition, nowadays, determines one's health and economic status. Hence, the quality of living conditions is used as an index of poverty. Hence, housing status, literacy and earning levels are considered to measure poverty.

Amartya Kumar Sen introduced another concept namely incidence of poverty, which is determined by the gap between one's income and the poverty level income. Longer the distance greater is the incidence. For instance if the poverty level income is Rs. 18,000 per annum if A's income is Rs. 17,000 and B's income is Rs. 15,000, the incidence of poverty is higher for B as compared to A.

While the quality of consumption determines the incidence of poverty, the quality of consumption itself is determined by various factors as identified by Keynes, Dusenbery, Jemes Tobin, Milton Friedman, Modigliani and others.

2.2 Definition of Households

Willard and Bell (1956) defined household as any unit, non-collective in form, which made choices with respect to the goods and services used in living, as a household. Thus the unit of household 'on the consumption side of the economy would be comparable with the unit of firm 'on the production side.

NCAER (1962) defined household, as a group of persons related by blood, marriage or adoption who would normally take meals from the same kitchen.

Sen (1973) stated a household as a group of persons, who commonly live together and would make their food from a common kitchen, unless the exigencies of work prevented any one of them from doing so.

Sidhu (1974) stated a household as a group of persons, at least some of them are interrelated, who live together and generally share a common kitchen. A single person is treated as a household provided that he (or) she maintains a kitchen.

As per NSSO (1989), household members are defined as persons who are normally residents of the sample household. Any person who lives and takes meals within the household is considered as a member of household.

Kailasam (1991) defined household as the one which consisted of a single economic decision making unit comprising of members, who were related to each other by blood, marriage, adoption or mutual understanding and lived in the same residence unit continuously, for not less than six months during the reference period, maintaining common accounts and sharing the same kitchen.

Sunitha, Aravind, Nalini, and Sundar (2007, 2008, 2010, and 2012) also defined household as a group of people related by blood and stayed together in the same house by maintaining common accounts on all types of income and expenditure incurred by common kitchen.

2.3 Definition of Employment

As per NSSO (1959), a person would be said to be fully employed if he worked for 42 hours or more in the reference week.

Bishnoi (1966) defined employment as a state of being engaged in productive activities. It should be continuous and non-intermittent and should have sufficient amount of man-hours or man-days of work and the income derived from it should be commensurate with the efforts made.

According to Sen (1973), employment is a state of being engaged in productive activities.

Vaidialingam (1980) opined that a person would be said to be fully employed if he worked for 300 days or more in one year.

Venkatram (2003) defined employment in monthly status. A person, who worked eight hours per day, considered as man-days which were grouped into employment for low and high income group for the less and well developed region of Tamil Nadu.

2.4 Income

Swenson and Jureen (1953) defined income as income from all sources including crops, other agricultural and non-agricultural sources and miscellaneous sources of income.

Malya (1961) defined gross income as the sum total of the income received by all the members of the household, from all sources besides income from main occupation, and dairy enterprises, rent received from leased out land, interest on loans and remittances.

NCAER (1962) defined income of a household as the earnings, both in cash and kind that occurred to and realized by the members of the household during the reference period of twelve months.

Batcheldar (1971) defined income as the amount that a household received as earning or from gifts during some period of time or between two points of time.

Nandal (1972) used the concept of farm family income consisting of farm income, non-farm income and borrowings.

NCAER (1989) defined household income as self-employment income from business, profession and services, salary, agricultural and non-agricultural wages, rent, interest and dividend income and transfer income.

Thilagavathi (1995) considered household income as the total amount of current receipts by all members of household, during the reference period, from wages and salaries, income from currently operating profession, services, rent, interest, dividend, gifts and bonds.

Jayakumar (1999) defined income as the sum total of income received by all members of the family members working in different categories or the same kind of work. He included income from all sources such as farm, non-farm and any assistance from government programmes.

Nalini (2010) defined income as the summation of on-farm income, off-farm income and non-farm income received by all members of the family during the reference period.

Sundar (2012) defined income as the summation of on-farm income, off-farm income and non-farm income received by all members of the family during the reference period.

For the present study income has been defined as the sum of income received by all members of the family working in different categories or the same kind of work. The sources of income included are farm, non-farm and any assistance from government programmes.

2.5 Definition of Consumption

NCAER (1962) defined consumption as all quantities purchased in exchange of money or goods and services or consumption of home-grown stocks, gifts or loans. Household consumption is referred to domestic consumption only and no account of the articles used by the household for production purpose was taken.

Yashwant (1963) stated that consumption expenditure included the expenditure on food, conventional necessities (i.e. tea, coffee, smoking, chewing etc.) fuel and lighting, housing and furniture's and miscellaneous expenditures (i.e. travelling, education, religious ceremonies, medicines, etc.).

According to NSSO (1989), household consumption expenditure comprised of all the expenditure incurred by the household on domestic account, including the consumption of home-grown products or transfer receipts like gifts and charities.

NCAER (1987) defined consumption expenditure as inclusive of expenditure on cereals, pulses, oils, oilseeds, milk and milk products, sweetening agent, spices, vegetables, refreshments, processed foods, biscuits, confectionaries, intoxicants, pawn, cigarettes, tobacco, fuel, light, cotton, wool, silk, clothing including readymade garments, rent for domestic purposes, amusements and sports, education, medicine, study goods and services, conveyance, ceremonies, gifts and miscellaneous current expenditure. It also included expenditure on consumer durables and semi durables, such as furniture, kitchen equipment‘s, insurance expenditure, license fees paid, expenditure on maintenance and repairs of various durables and semi durables.

Gopalakrishnan (1993) defined consumption as the expenses on non-durable goods and services used up and the annual cost (deprecation, plus interest cost less if any) of durable goods.

Jayakumar (1999) defined consumption as the total consumption expenditure which included food, fuel, shelter, medical, recreation, beverages and narcotics, social, dresses, education and other miscellaneous expenditures.

Balamurugan and Iyyampillai (2005) concluded that the rise in per capita income particularly of the middle class resulted in a drastic change in the food habits and led to an increased domestic consumption of processed fruits and vegetables.

Aravind (2008) stated that consumption has been defined as total consumption expenditure on food, clothing, shelter, education, recreation, transport, ceremonies, religious activities, beverages and narcotics, medicine and other miscellaneous expenditure.

Sivasakthidevi (2010) opined that consumption could be referred as expenditure on food items and non-food items such as clothing, education, rent, fuel, electricity charges, mobile and petrol charges for vehicle, transport, ceremonies, religious activities, beverages and narcotics, medicine and other miscellaneous expenditure.

Nalini (2010) defined consumption expenditure as total amount of money spent in household in a reference year on food items and non-food items such as clothing, shelter, education, recreation, transport, ceremonies, religious activities, beverages and narcotics, medicine and other miscellaneous expenditure.

Sundar (2012) defined consumption as total consumption expenditure on food, clothing, shelter, education, recreation, transport, ceremonies, religious activities, beverages and narcotics, medicine and other miscellaneous expenditure.

2.6 Definition of Poverty

Friedman (1960) defined poverty as a form of disempowerment along three dimensions; *viz.*, social, political and psychological. Social referred to poor people‘s relative lack of access to resources essential for the self-production of their livelihood, political referred to poor people‘s lack of clear political agenda and psychological referred to poor people‘s internalized sense of worthlessness.

Pant (1980) explained the concept of poverty in a broader perspective and included not only those who were unemployed and poor, but also those who were fully or partly exploited but earned very little because of low productivity and low wages.

United Nations (1995) defined Absolute poverty [as] a condition characterized by severe deprivation of basic human needs, including food, safe drinking water, sanitation facilities, health, shelter, education and information. It depends not only on income but also on access to social services

Datt and Sundharam (1998) defined poverty as a special phenomenon in which a section of the society failed to fulfill even its basic necessities of life.

Sen (1999) further developed this argument by emphasizing that 'real' poverty can be defined in terms of 'capability deprivation,' which refers to deprivation of opportunities, choice and entitlements.

Bourguignon and Chakravarty (2003) it is increasingly recognized that monetary measures of income or expenditure provide only partial insights into standards of living or well-being. Many researchers have noted that poverty is multidimensional, reflecting a range of deprivations.

The Planning Commission (2010) used data on household consumer expenditure (based on the 66th round of the National Sample Survey in 2009–10) to estimate that the proportion of poor people in India was 29.8 per cent in 2009–10, down from 37.2 per cent in 2004–5. However, a large number of Indians continue to live in poverty and disparities in income and human development are on the rise.

According to India's Economic Survey 2012-13, totally 233.33 million jobs were lost in agricultural and 4.2 million jobs in manufacturing over the period 2004-05 and 2009-10.

Chandrasekhar's (2014) study stated that in rural India, the average monthly per capita consumption expenditure (MPCE) of households was lower than Rs. 601.

2.7 Poverty Related Studies

Ojha (1970) estimated the number of persons BPL on the basis of an average calorie intake of 2250 per capita per day. On this basis, he estimated that 184 million persons in the rural areas (51.80 per cent) and six million persons in the urban areas (7.60 per cent) lived BPL. For the country as a whole, 190 million persons (44.00 per cent) could be classified as poor in 1960-61.

Dandekar and Rath (1971) estimated that about 40 per cent of the rural population (166 million) and 50 per cent of urban population (49 million) lived below poverty line by using Head Count Ratio. The total number of persons below the poverty line was 41 per cent (215 million).

Ahluwalia (1978) estimated the incidence of rural poverty in India for the period from 1956-57 to 1973-74 using an expenditure level of Rs. 15 in 1960-61 prices for rural areas and Rs.20 per person per month for urban areas. The results showed that in 1956-57, 181 million persons (54.10 per cent) lived BPL in rural areas whereas it was 24 million persons (46.10 per cent) in 1973-74.

Atul Goswami's (1984) study reveled that the tribal populations are grossly deficient in infrastructural facilities, suffer from land alienation, land fragmentation and outmoded agricultural practices, those are the reason for the tribals living BPL.

Ahluwalia (1986) studied the trend of poverty for a period from 1956-57 to 1977-78. The results obtained by regression both the poverty ratio (Head Count Measure) and the Sen Index of poverty on time showed that there is no underlying time trend in poverty for the period as a whole. The percentage of the population in poverty declined though the fifties rose to a peak in 1967-68 and then declined substantially though unevenly through seventies.

Datt and Ravillion (1989) developed the concept of poverty gap along with the poverty line. They used Rs.89 per month per person as the poverty line and used rural interstate price relatives (ratio of rural prices in a state to all India prices) for 1973-74 and updated to 1983 using consumer price index for agricultural laborers as the rural price deflator. Similarly, consumer price index for industrial workers has been used to update the inter-state price relatives for urban areas. They found out that 90 per cent of the population was BPL among them 40.00 per cent lived in urban and 45.00 per cent lived in rural areas.

Garcia *et al.* (2000) used head count ratio, poverty gap ratio and squared poverty gap ratio to measure incidence, intensity and severity of poverty in different ecosystem (irrigated and rainfed) in Myanmar. The study reveals that the head count ratio was higher in the irrigated villages (35 per cent) than in the rain fed villages (21 per cent). Further they found that households in irrigated villages were worse off in terms of income generation compared with those in rain fed villages.

Anderson (2003) estimated poverty in the Mexican Border States. The study showed that poverty decreased from 1970 to 2000 in all states except Sonora. The states that experienced the highest decrease in poverty rates were Coahuila (from 66.3 per cent to 51.8 per cent); Baja California (from 55.3 per cent to 41.7 per cent) and Chihuahua (from 62.1 per cent to 50.9 per cent).

Kundu and Sarangi (2007) analyzed poverty and migration pattern across urban areas based on the data from 55th round of National Sample Survey (NSS). The results indicated that the probability of being poor is much less among the migrants compared to the local population, in all size classes of urban centers.

Dev and Ravi (2007) studied poverty and inequality among the states in India by using National Sample Survey data (61st round, 2004-05) over the period 1983-2005. The results revealed that the total poverty ratio based on uniform reference period declined by 0.85 percentage points per annum in the pre-reform period (1983-94) and 0.70 percentage points in the post-reform period (1994-05). In case of mixed reference period for the two sub-periods, the rate of decline in the second period (1999-05) was higher (1.02 percentage points) as compared to the first period (0.69 percentage points.).

Himanshu (2007) examined poverty during the period 1993 to 2005 by using uniform reference period data on consumption expenditure. The results revealed that the poverty had come down in all states during 1993-94 and 2004-05, but the annual poverty reduction is slower than in the previous decade of 1983 to 19993-94.

Alkire and Seth (2008) estimated BPL headcount by using India‘s 2002 census data. By using the BPL 2002 methodology and NFHS (National Family Health Survey) data, the results revealed that up to 12 per cent of the poor sample population and 33 per cent of the extreme poor could be misclassified as non-poor by the pseudo-BPL method.

Tendulkar Committee (2009-10) uses the norm of Rs.447 & Rs.579 per capita per month for rural and urban area based on minimum calorie requirements of 2100 calorie for rural and 1776 calorie for urban for defining poverty line in India.

The Rangarajan Committee (2012) computed the average requirements of calories of 2,155 kcal per person per day in rural and urban 2,090 kcal per person per day. The Committee finds out 30.9% &

26.4% population below the poverty line in rural and urban areas and 29.5% in over all India.

The World Bank (2013) recently estimates that 10.7 percent of world population are living or below poverty line in money term ($1.90 a day).

2.8 Employment and income studies

Manas Das Gupta (1984) stated that households income is spent on agricultural, social services like education, health care, child care, community education, etc.

Thilagavathi (1995) analysed the impact of operation flood on income and employment generation to rural women in Madurai district of Tamil Nadu. The results revealed that in areas where the operation flood progarmme was operated, the employment created for the women folk in the rural areas was nearly double, livestock enterprises created nearly 286 days of employment of rural women in the beneficiary households as compared to 142 days for non-beneficiary households. The income from livestock per family was Rs. 18,792 and Rs. 1,783 respectively for beneficiaries and non-beneficiaries respectively implying that livestock was one of the major components of the income-generating source for the rural families.

Gopalappa (1996) analysed the effect of agricultural diversification on the income and standard of living of the farmers over time. The results revealed that the average income per month per household was Rs. 876 for the marginal and Rs. 1,843 for the small farm households for the same land holding before taking up sericulture. However, after introduction of sericulture, the average farm income per month had increased to Rs.2, 402 and Rs. 3,280 in the marginal and small farms, respectively.

The study by Basanta K. Pradhan, P. K Ray, M. R. Saluja and Shanta Venkaram (2000) reveled that rural households income to go down during the last two decades, at the same time the wide disparities in income distribution between rural and urban areas through the India.

Ponnarasi (2000) analyzed the employment pattern, income distribution and poverty levels in varying irrigation environments of Coimbatore district. The study on employment pattern revealed that the average number of days employed per month in irrigated block was 25 days as against 21 days in dry block. The number of days per month employed in lean season was 21 days for irrigated block and 18 days for dry block. The average annual income earned from on farm, off- farm and non-farm employment by the respondents in irrigated block were Rs.15304.39, Rs.7887.88 and Rs.15311.93 respectively. Similarly, in dry block the income realized was Rs.15732.47, Rs.5635.02 and Rs.17992.50 per annum from on-farm off-farm and non-farm employment respectively. The income distribution among sample respondents showed that inequality was moderate in dry block than in irrigated block.

The study by Basanta K. Pradhan, P. K Ray, M. R. Saluja and Shanta Venkaram (2000) express that in agricultural wage earning households, consumption expenditure is the highest (61 per cent), followed by self-employed farm and non-agricultural wage earning households (55 per cent) in rural area through the India.

Deaton and Dreze (2002) stated that healthy growth in real agricultural wages appears to be a sufficient condition for significant reduction in poverty in rural areas. The growth of regular wage during the per-and post reform period almost same in rural areas. Sundaram K (2003) found that among the economic groups, those who are dependent on casual daily wage labour in an environment of uncertain and fluctuating employment (agricultural labour households) report the highest levels of poverty in rural India.

Mahabub Hossain's (2004) study analyses the share of non-agriculture income in rural household increased from 36 per cent to 42 per cent in 1982 to 1987, again it has increased 52 per cent in 2000. The result also shows that increasing trend in rural non-agricultural employment opportunities has go for 34 to 52 per cent in 1987-2000.

Aravind (2008) depicted the average number of days employed per month for agriculturalists, agricultural laborers, other workers in Dharmapuri district of Tamil Nadu. He also stated that in Morappur and Nallampalli blocks, the average number of days employed per month was 19 and 16 days respectively. The income earned in Morappur and

Nallampalli block was about Rs.49846.33 and Rs.33013.89 respectively from on farm, off farm and non-farm per annum respectively.

Mahendra Dev et.al (2010) estimated that bottom 30 per cent of the population in rural and urban areas still incurred 66 and 60 per cent respectively on their total expenditure on food items. In this context the recent increase in food prices is major cause of concern for the poor and the very poor who are still continuing below poverty line.

The study by Mahendra Dev et.al (2010) recommended to creating of employment opportunity for both rural and urban areas it as ensuring that increasing household income, increasing purchasing power of poor people and able to met their food consumption in whole year.

Sundar's (2012) study found that majority of the peoples monthly income ranges between Rs.1000-2000. Only very small percentage of the population gets assistance from the government and it is due to the fact that most of the tribes were not aware about the government assistance.

According to Prem Nazeer C (2015) the majority of the tribes of the Pachamalai hill belong to nuclear family and majority of them were uneducated. The economic conditions of the tribes primarily depended on agriculture, forest and labouring. Similarly, it was found that majority (50%) of the people do agriculture and 25 percent of them were engaged in forest work. It was found that majority of the peoples monthly income ranges between Rs.1,000-2,000. Only very small percentage of the population get assistance from the government and it is due to the fact that most of the tribes were not aware about the government assistance.

Swarnam, Velmurugan and Saravana Kumar (2015) in their study show that for the island tribal community sale of copra was the major source of income for majority of the households. One-third of households have income received from non-farm activities like government service. The same way one-third of total income was spend on religious ceremonies and children's marriage household.

The study by Elisa Wildayana, Imanudin, Junedi, Mohd, Zuhdi, Edi Armanto (2016) the study shows that the household income has increased because of increase in agricultural yields.

Meena (2017) analyses tribal households income of Jharkhand this study shows a huge difference (8, 493) in per capita income among households per annum. For many tribal households non-farm activity is a major share of income.

2.9 Studies on Poverty in Tribal Population

As compared to other groups of populations, the economic poverty appears to be higher among the Tribal Population. The reasons are obvious. They are away from economic systems; they give least importance for economic status; they engage in work not on the basis of remuneration; the choice is very few, the technologies are traditional and so on.

Sivakumar (1976) shows that changing household consumption expenditure, income and occupation directly depend on the landholding size, more land they get more income and less consumption expenditure. less landholding there income has less but consumption expenditure was high, at the same time they are seasonally shift to non-agricultural work in the rural areas.

Reddy KN (1976) has estimated that inter- state deference in per capita consumption expenditure. He found that large gab in monthly per capita expenditures in the states, like Uttar Pradesh Rs. 48.34, Kashmir Rs. 151.42, Tamil Nadu Rs. 84.88 and Kerala Rs. 82.88. This compared to tribal area is very low in Tamil Nadu.

Bhalerao and Gupta (1984) attempted to analyse the income and employment among the Gond and Korku tribal with the help of a micro enquiry in a predominantly tribal area. The studies found that there are considerable inter-tribal and inter group variation in employment and income of the households in tribal area.

The study by Vijay Nayak and Shalaja Prasad (1984) analyses that the mean consumption expenditure of the SCs/STs wide gap in compared to non-SCs/STs household in rural area. But the there not much deferent in the consumption expenditure in SCs households and STs households in rural areas.

The analysis of Vijay Nayak and Shalaja Prasad (1984) shows that 54. 8 per cent of non-SCs/STs and 79.9 per cent of SCs/STs population are living in below poverty line in rural areas, followed by urban area

50.4 and 63.6 per cent of non-SCs/STs and SCs/STs population are living in below poverty line in Karnataka state.

Bhattaacharya and Lakshmanaiah (1992) revealed that the states namely Nagaland and Meghalaya were not required to draw up a separate sub-plan for tribal welfare as the other states do. It is so because Nagaland and Meghalaya are concentrated by STs, and hence their whole plane is a tribal plan.

Padmaja Mishra (1992) analyses the NSSO data for decomposing expenditure in 1977-78 and 1983, he find out overall inequality will be reduced exactly by 5.3 per cent as measured by decomposing methods, at the same time he did not mention that how much total inequality was reduced.

Ninan KN (1994) estimated that rural household's income on the basis of US $, and found that around 422 million of people are absolutely poor in 1985.

Meenakshi and Ranjan's (2002) study pointed out rural household consumption expenditure of cereals and pulses product, milk and milk product, meat, cloths and other non-food items of per capita expenditure Rs. 309.22 in average household size was 4.04 on non- SCs and STs. In SCs and STs Households expenditure was Rs. 252.6 household size was 4.03, this study clearly shows that tribal community population are still livings below poverty line.

Sujith Kumar (2007) has found that 53 per cent of rural household generated income from agricultural sector. Landless households earn more than 59 per cent of total income from non-agricultural households. Sundare Rao (2012) observed that about 53 per cent of the households are living BPL. The majority of the households APL are also not significantly better off than the households in BPL.

Madura Swaminathan (2008) observed around one-third of total rural households income are derived from the non-fram sector, among the economically and socially deprived section of the rural population.

Geetha (2011) estimated consumption patterns among Selected Rural and Urban Households in Coimbatore district. The study found the significant differentials in consumption expenditure not only between the groups (rural vs. urban) but also within the group also. Low consumption expenditure elasticity for cereals and higher consumption expenditure elasticity for other food items signifies a shifting food consumption pattern in both rural and urban areas as income increases.

Prdhan and Sethi (2012) estimated the average income and expenditure of rural households in Odisha. The study found that Rs. 75,358 average income of households, the average consumption expenditure on food for all the households was 24,854 and non-food Rs. 34,637 followed by average expenditure households Rs. 59,491 the consumption ratio 0.80 for all the households.

The study by Narayan Sethi and Hemanta Kumar Phadhan (2012) shows that the tribal population spend more income on food consumption like cereals, egg, fish, chicken, tobacco products, and intoxicants etc, but less on milk and milk products, fruits and refreshments, followed by non-food expenditure like education, health, clothing etc. also.

Pratap (2012) analysed the pattern of land and livestock. According to him tribal population are holding more livestock for their livelihood.

Kiran Kumar B Dhanappa (2013) has studied the food consumptions pattern of Malayali tribal population. In their food, 35 per cent is millets, 10 per cent is maize and 5 per cent is wheat.

Sethia (2013) study found that Indian consumption patterns are changing and that the share of food items in total aggregate consumption expenditure declined from 53.7 per cent in 1970-71 to 48.4 per cent. In the food consumption expenditure was declined from 49.9 per cent in 1991-92 to 35.4 per cent in 2004-2005.

Planning Commission (2013) released the poverty estimates based on the 2009–2010 expenditure survey. The Planning Commission reported the average poverty lines as Rs28.26 and Rs22.2 per person per day in urban and rural areas respectively.

Kamini's (2013) study shows that higher income households spend less amount on their food expenditure, low income households 90 per cent of total income on food expenditure, and those who have attained higher level of education spend less amount on spend food consumption in her study area.

Pratap and Birthal (2014) found that 91 per cent of households reported 41 .4 per cent of income received from agricultural activities.

24.4 per cent of household income received from non-frame income sources.

UNDESA's (2015) the Millennium Development Goals (MDGs) report says, 1990 and 2015 end of the goals 1 billion people have overcome the poverty around the world.

Anju Bala's (2018) study noted that main reasons for the poverty, indebtedness of tribal population, are old mode of agricultural practices, ignorance, low production, and loss of tribal rights over land and forest.

2.10 Tribal development related studies

The important things in the tribal welfare schemes are to understand the problem of the tribal population. The main problems of tribal are isolation from the rest of population. Further, the welfare schemes aimed at the alleviation of poverty, providing them literacy and prevent them from the exploitation by the other population.

According to Vidyarthi (1968) after Independence, the Government of India followed a tribal policy formulated by the British model in slightly modified. After a decade due to constant thinking of social reforms, Politian's and anthropologists evolved a desirable course for the integration of the tribal population.

Atul Goswami's (1984) study result shows that tribal are getting additional infrastructural facilities like education, transport, communication facilities, health and hygiene, creating irrigation facilities and specific family oriented schemes would be help for uplift of below poverty line for the tribal population.

The Dhebar Commission stated that land, forest, livestock, cottage and village industries should be integrated, then only the tribal problems can be solved.

The tribal situation was again reviewed during The Fifth Five Year Plan (1974-79). The Planning Commission of India accelerates the objective of SCs/STs development, and reduction in poverty and unemployment, creation of productive assets and income generating opportunities, human resource development like education, health services and improving quality of life by providing house, basic amenities in SCs/STs. Through the Tribal-Sub-Plan (TSP) for out of 17 states and included Tamil Nadu (Hutton 1963).

According to Singh (2006) the Government of India allotted funds through the Five Year Plans for tribal welfare. The Government introduced the Tribal Development Programme in the area of education, reservation in employment, providing health care facilities, housing, credit, communication, drinking water facility for the tribal areas. The Malayalis of Jawadhu hill, Kolli hills, Pachaimalai and Kalrayan hills, Servaran hills were listed twenty fifth in the list of Scheduled Tribes.

As per Harishankar Banothu (2016) tribal development schemes have not brought any changes in the life of mainstream of the tribal people. Inclusive growth is not making the fruits of development available and accessible to the tribal population in grass rout level of India.

References:

Ahluwalia, M. S. (1978): "Rural Poverty and Agricultural Performance in India," Journal of Development Studies, 14(3), pp. 298-303.

Ahluwalia, M. S. (1986): "Rural Poverty Agricultural Production and Prices: A Re-examination in Agricultural Change and Rural Poverty Variations on a Theme by Dharm Narain, John W. Mellor & Gunwant Desal (eds.), Oxford University Press, Bombay.

Alkire, S., and Seth, S. (2008): "Multidimensional Poverty Measurement and BPL Methods in India: A Comparison of Methods," Oxford University: Oxford Poverty and Human Development Initiative, (Working Paper No15).

Anderson, J. B. (2003): "The U.S.-Mexico Border: A Half Century of Change," Social Science Journal, Vol. 40 (4), pp. 535-554.

Anju Bala (2018): "Tribes in India: The regional analysis," International Journal of Advanced Research and Development, Volume 3, Issue 1, pp. 54-57.

Aravind K. R. (2008): "An Economic Analysis of Poverty and Livelihood Security among Rural Households in Dharmapuri District of Tamil Nadu," Unpublished M.Sc.(Ag.) Thesis submitted to Department of Agricultural Economics, Tamil Nadu Agricultural University, Coimbatore.

Atul Goswami (1984): "Tribal Development with Special Reference to North-East India," Social Scientist, Vol. 12, No. 8, pp. 55-60.

Balamurugan, P. & Iyyampillai, S. (2005): "Fruit and Vegetable Processing Industry: Some Issues," Southern Economist, 44(12), pp. 21-23.

Batcheldar (1971): "The Economics of Poverty," John Willey and Sons Publications, New York.

Batcheldar (1971): "The Economics of Poverty," John Willey and Sons Publications, New York.

Basanta K. Pradhan, P. K Ray, M. R. Saluja and Shanta Venkaram (2000): "Rural-Urban Disparities: Income Distribution, Expenditure Pattern and Social Sector," Economic and Political Weekly, Vol. 35, No. 28/29, pp. 2527-2529+2531-2539.

Bishnoi (1966): "Pattern of Employment and Nature and Causes of Unemployment in Agriculture," Indian Journal of Agricultural Economics, 21(1), pp. 51-61.

Bourguignon, F. and Chakravarty (2003): "The Measurement of Multidimensional Poverty," Journal of Economic Inequality, Vol. 1, pp. 25–49.

Chandrasekhar, Mousumi Das and Ajay Sharma (2014): "Short-term Migration and Consumption Expenditure of Households in Rural India," Indira Gandhi Institute of Development Research, Mumbai. http://www.igidr.ac.in/pdf/publication/WP-2014-009.pdf. accessed data, 25-10-2016.

Dandekar, V. M., & Rath, R. (1971): "Poverty in India, Dimensions and Trends." Economic and Political Weekly, Vol.6, No. 1, pp. 25-48.

Deaton and Dreze (2002): "Poverty and Inequality in India: A Re-Examination," Economic and Political Weekly, Vol. 37, pp. 3729-3748.

Datt, G., and Ravillion, M. (1989): "Region Disparities, Targetion and Poverty in India," World Bank, (Paper W.P.S, 375).

Datt, R., & Sundharam, K. P. M. (1998): "Indian Economy," S Chand and Company, New Delhi.

Dev, S. M., and Ravi, C. (2007): "Poverty and Inequality: All India and States 1983-2005," Economic and Political Weekly, Vol. 42(6), pp. 509-521.

Elisa Wildayana, Imanudin, Junedi, Mohd, Zuhdi, Edi Armanto (2016): "Parameters Affecting Household Income Diversity of Farmer's Tribes in South Sumatra Tidal Wetland," Sriwijaya journal of Environment,Vol. 1 No. 3, pp. 47-52.

Friedmann, J. (1960): "Rethinking Poverty: Empowerment and Citizen Rights," International Social Science Journal, 48(148), pp. 161-172.

Garcia, Y T., Garcia, A. G., M., and Hossain, M. (2000): "Income Distribution and Poverty in Irrigated and Rain fed Ecosystem; The Myanmar Case," Economic and Political Weekly, Vol. 35(52/53), pp. 4670-4676.

Geetha. K.T. (2011): "Consumption Patterns Among Selected Rural and Urban Households in Coimbatore City," International Journal of Multidisciplinary Research, vol. 1, issue 2, pp 46-60.

George, S. (1994): "Tribal Development; Legislation Enforcement," New Delhi, 1994, pp.47.

Gopalakrishnan (1993): "A Study of Consumption and Pattern Deviation," Unpublished M.Sc. (Ag.) Thesis submitted to Department of Agricultural Economics, Tamil Nadu Agricultural University, Coimbatore.

Harishankar Banothu (2016): "Tribal Economic Development in India," International Journal of Multidisciplinary Advanced Research Trends Issn: 2349-7408 Volume (III), Issue 1(3), pp.28-34.

Himanshu. (2007): "Recent Trends in Poverty and Inequality: Some Preliminary Results," Economic and Political Weekly, Vol. 42(6), pp. 497-508.

Jayakumar, P. N. (1999): "A Micro Level Study on Poverty and Food Insecurity of Rural Households in Kanchipuram District of Tamil Nadu," Unpublished M.Sc. (Ag.) Thesis submitted to Department of Agricultural Economics, Tamil Nadu Agricultural University, Coimbatore.

Kailasam (1991): "An Econometric Study of Complete Demand System for Rural and Urban Households in Western Tamil Nadu," Unpublished M.Sc. (Ag.) Thesis submitted to Department of Agricultural Economics, Tamil Nadu Agricultural University, Coimbatore.

KiranKumar B Dhanappa (2013): "Prevalence of Malocclusion Among Malayali Tribes at Javadu Hills in Polur Taluka, Tamilnadu," Journal of research and advancement in dentistry, pp.38-43. ISSN2278-0076.

Kundu, A., and Sarangi, N. (2007): "Migration, Employment Status and Poverty: An Analysis Across Urban Centers," Economic and Political Weekly, Vol. 42(4), pp. 299-306.

Mahabub Hossain (2004): "Rural Non-Farm Economy, Evidence from Household Survey," Economic and Political Weekly, Vol, XXXIX, No.36, Sep. pp.4053 -4058.

Mahendra Dev et.al (2010): "Food security in India performance, Challenges and polices," Oxfam India working paper series, Oxfam India, New Delhi.

Malya (1961): "An Analysis of Personal Income Distribution in Rural Areas," Indian Journal of Agricultural Economics, 16(1), pp. 187-195.

Manas Das Gupta (1984): "Tribal unrest," Economic and political weekly, Vol. 19, No. 11, PP 449-451.

Meenakshi and Ranjan Ray (2002): "Impact of household size and family composition on poverty in rural India," Journal of Policy Modeling, pp. 539-559.

Ministry of Trible Affairs annual report (2008-09): Government of India, New Delhi Pg. 167.

M S Meena, K M Singh, R K P Singh, Anjani Kumar, Abhay Kumar and V P Chahal (2017): "Inequality and determinants of income among rural households in tribal dominated areas of Jharkhand," Indian Journal of Agricultural Sciences 87 (1): 92–96.

Nadeem Hasnain (2007): "Tribal India," Palka Prakashan publication, New Delhi. Pg. 378.

Nalini, T. (2010): "An economic assessment of Agricultural and livelihood security among the rural households in Karnataka state," Unpublished M.Sc. (Ag.) Thesis submitted to Department of Agricultural Economics, Tamil Nadu Agricultural University, Coimbatore.

Nandal (1972): "Pattern of Income Investment Expenditure and Savings of Selected Demonstration Farms in Haryana," Indian Journal of Agricultural Economics, 27(4), pp. 11-19.

Narayan Sethi and Hemanta Kumar Phadhan (2012): "The Patterns of Consumption expenditure in Rural Households of Western Odisha of India: An Engel Ratio Analysis," Ontario International development Agency, ISSN: 1923-6654, pp. 117-128.

NCAER (1962): "Long Term Projects of Demand for the Supply of Selected Agricultural Commodities, 1960-61 to 1975-76," National Council of Applied Economic Research, New Delhi.

NCAER. (1989): "Household Income and Its Disposition," National Council of Applied Economic Research, New Delhi.

Ninan. KN (1994): "Poverty and income distributions," Economic and political weekly, pp. 1544-1551.

NSSO (1959): "Note in the Consumer Expenditure Survey," National Sample Survey organization, New Delhi.

NSSO (1989): "Note in the Consumers Expenditure Survey 42nd Round," National Sample Survey organization, New Delhi.

Ojha, P. D. (1970): "A Configuration of Indian Poverty – Inequality and Level of Living Challenges of Poverty in India," Reserve Bank of India Bulletin, 24(1), pp. 16-27.

Padmaja Mishra (1992): "Household consumer expenditure inequalities in India: A decomposition analysis," Review of income and wealth, series 38, no.2, pp.225-236.

Pant, S. P. (1980): "Poverty, Unemployment and Food for Work," Agricultural Situation in India, 35(2), pp. 83-90.

Planning Commission (1992): "Eight Five Year Plan 1992-97," Government of India, New Delhi.

Planning commission reports (2009-10, 2011-12): Government of India, New Delhi.

Ponnarasi, T. (2000): "An Economic Analysis of Employment, Income Distribution and Poverty Levels in Varying Irrigation Environs of Coimbatore District," Unpublished M.Sc. (Ag.) Thesis submitted to Department of Agricultural Economics, Tamil Nadu Agricultural University, Coimbatore.

Pradhan and Sethi (2012): "The pattern of consumption expenditure in rural households of Western Odisha of India: An Engel ratio analysis," ODIA international journal of sustainable development, ISSN 1923-6662 (online), available at http:www.ssrn.com/link/ODIA-intl-journal-sustainable-dve.html. pp107-128.

Prabakaran, R. Senthil Kumar,T. and Rao, V.M (2013): "Role of Non-Timber Forest Products in the Livelihood of Malayali Tribe of Chitteri hills of Southern Eastern Ghats, Tamil Nadu, India," Journal of Applied Pharmaceutical science, Vol.3 (05), pp. 056-060.

Pratap (2012): "Livestock for higher, sustainable and inclusive agricultural growth," Economics and political weekly, Vol. XLVII, No. 26-27, pp. 89-98

Pratap and Birthal (2014): "Income sources of farm household in India: Determinates distributional consequences and policy implications," Agricultural Economics Research Review, Vol.27, No.1, pp 37-48.

Prem Nazeer (2015): "Tribals in Tamil Nadu with Special Reference to Tribes of Pachamalai Hills," Historical Research Letter, ISSN 2224-3178 (Paper) ISSN 2225-0964 (Online) Vol 18.

Reddy (1976): "Inter-state differences in social consumption," Economic and political weekly, Vol. 11, No. 24, pp. 872-879.

Thilagavathi, M. (1995): "Impact of Operation Flood on Income and Employment Level in Rural Women – A Study in Madurai District," Unpublished M.Sc. (Ag.) Thesis submitted to Department of Agricultural Economics, Tamil Nadu Agricultural University, Coimbatore.

Sanghamitra Kannongo (2011): "Tribal and Human Rights," Delhi, pp.83-86.

Sen, A. K. (1973): "Employment Policy and Technological Choice," Oxford University Press, London.

Sen, A. K. (1976): "Poverty: An Ordinal Approach to Measurement," Econometrica, Vol. 44(2), pp. 219-231.

Sen, A. (1999): "Development as Freedom," Anchor Books Publishing Company, New York.

Sidhu (1974): "On the Economic Inequality Statistics Canada," Oxford: Clarendum press, pp. 205-210.

Singh, K.S (2006): "The Scheduled Tribe," Vol. III, Chennai, pp.736.

Sethia Savneet. (2013): "India's Changing Consumption Pattern," Gyanpratha-Accman Journal of Management, volume 5, issue 2.

Sivasakthidevi (2010): "Rural Employment Generation Programmes Vs Food Subsidy Programmes- An Economic Analysis of Household Employment, Consumption and Welfare in Tamil Nadu," Unpublished M.Sc. (Ag.) Thesis submitted to Department of Agricultural Economics, Tamil Nadu Agricultural University, Coimbatore.

Sivakumar (1976): "Family size consumption expenditure, income, and land holding on agrarian economy: A Critique of some populist nation," Economic and Political Weekly, Vol. 11, No,30, pp.1115+1117-1124.

Sundar, A. (2012): "Impact of Mahathma Gandhi National Rural Employment Guarantee Programme (MGNREGs) On Rural Households of Sivagangai Distrct of Tamil Nadu: An Economic Analysis," Unpublished Ph.D Thesis submitted to Department of Agricultural Economics, Tamil Nadu Agricultural University, Coimbatore.

Sundara Rao (2012): "Determinants Of Poverty In Tribal Households In Andhra Pradesh (A Study On Visakhapatnam District," International Journal Of Multidisciplinary Educational Research, ISSN: 2277-7881, Volume 1, Issue 2, pp-38-46.

Sundram (2003): "Poverty among social and economic groups in India in 1990," Economic and political weekly, Vol. 38, No. 50, pp. 5263-5276

Sunitha A. (2007): "An Economic Analysis of Urban Food Consumption in Coimbatore city," Unpublished M.Sc. (Ag.) Thesis submitted to Department of Agricultural Economics, Tamil Nadu Agricultural University, Coimbatore

Swarnam, Velmurugan and Saravana Kumar (2015): "Studies on Tribal Farming in Nicobar Islands, India," IOSR Journal of Agriculture and Veterinary Science (IOSR-JAVS), Volume 8, Issue 1 Ver. II (Jan. 2015), PP 41-49.

Swenson & Jureen (1953): "Demand Analysis: A Study in Econometrics," John Willey and Sons Publications, New York.

United Nations. (1995): "Report of the World Summit for Social Development," accessed from http://www.un.org/esa/socdev/docs/summit.pdf.

United Nations (2013): "State of the World's Indigenous Peoples."

Vaidialingam (1980): "A Study on Employment, Income and Expenditure pattern of Landless Labour and Rural Artisans," Unpublished M.Sc. (Ag.) Thesis submitted to Department of Agricultural Economics, Tamil Nadu Agricultural University Coimbatore.

Venkatram (2003): "Assessment of food Security in Rural households – A study in Southern Tamil Nadu," Unpublished M.Sc. (Ag.) Thesis submitted to Department of Agricultural Economics, Tamil Nadu Agricultural University, Coimbatore.

Vidyarthi, L.P. and Rai, B.K. (1960): "The Tribal Culture of India," Delhi, pp.412.

Vijay Nayak and Shalaja Prasad (1984): "On Level of Living of Scheduled Castes and Scheduled Tribes," Economic and Political Weekly, Vol. 19, No. 30, pp.1205-1213.

Willard & Bell (1956): "The Economics of Consumption and Economics of Decision Mainly in the Households," McGraw Hill Book Company, New York.

World Bank (2007): "Jharkhand: Addressing the Challenges of Inclusive Development," Report No. 36437-IN Poverty Reduction and Economic Management. India Country Management Unit, South.

Yashwant (1963): "Income and Levels in Some South India Villages," Indian Journal of Agricultural Economics, 18(1), pp. 302.

Zalak Shah (2013): "The Income and Expenditure Pattern of Families at the Bottom of the Pyramid," Unpublished research work, accessed by Google scholar.

Websites:

http://www.tn.gov.in/scheme. Accessed data 25-09-2017.

http://asiancenturyinstitute.com/society/804-asia-s-indigenous-peoplesAccessed 12-09-2017.

Chapter III

Tribal Development

3.1 Introduction

The British government adopted the policy of isolation and tried to keep the tribals away from the mainstream of India. The British government found some places come under the Scheduled District Act in 1874 and administratively separated the tribal areas. The same situation was allowed to continue under the Government of India Act of 1919 and 1935. However, after Independence, this policy was abandoned and a new policy of tribal development and integration was initiated.

The former Prime Minister Jawaharlal Nehru formulated a state policy towards tribal development. The policy aimed at providing an enabling framework for the tribal people to move according to their own gene in a system of self-governance while sharing the benefits of development retaining the best elements of their tradition, cultural of life. The fundamental principle of tribal development laid down by Jawaharlal Nehru.

1. Tribal people should develop along the line of their own gene and we should avoid imposing anything on them. We must try to encourage in every way, their-own traditional arts and culture.
2. Tribal people is rights in land forest should be respected.
3. We must try to train and build up a team of their own people to do the work of administrative and development. Some technical personnel from outside will no doubt be needed especially in the beginning. But we must avoid introducing too many outsiders in tribal territory.
4. We must not over administer these areas or overwhelm them with a multiplicity of schemes. We must rather work through and not in rivalry to their own social and cultural institutions.

Based on these principles the Constitution of India has made special provision for the welfare and uplift of the tribal people throughout the country. The Articles 15 (4) 46, 244 (1) and 339 of Indian constitution provide special provision and rights.

3.2 Tribal development polices and programmes

The Government of India appointed a number of commissions and committees to look at the problems of development of tribal areas in the country. Hence they also recommended, removing the socio-economic imbalances and breaking down their old psychological barriers in tribal areas. List of commissions and committees are below.

1. The Social Welfare Team of the Committee on Plan Projects - 1959.
2. The Verrier Elwin committee on Tribal Development.
3. The Scheduled Areas and Scheduled Tribal Commission (Dhebar Committee)-1961.
4. The Special Working Group on Cooperatives for Backward Classes-1961 (Shri M.D. Bhargava as its chairman).
5. The Committee on Tribal Economy in Forest Areas-1967.
6. The Task Forces on Development of Tribal Areas- 1972.
7. The Dube Committee- 1972.
8. The Study Group on Relief of Indebtedness Land Alienation and Restoration in Development Agency Area- 1973 (Shri P.S. Appu as its Chairman).
9. The Study Team on Co-operative Structure in Tribal Development Project Area- 1976.
10. The Team of Marketing, Credit, and Cooperation in Tribal Areas- 1978.
11. The Working Group on Development of Scheduled Tribes During the Seventh Five Year Plan -1985-90.
12. The Planning Commission constituted in 2010 a Task Force under the Chairmanship of Narendra Jadhav, Member, Planning Commission, to review the operational difficulties in implementing TSP/SCSP

Several commissions and committees gave several recommendations and suggestions. The major suggestions are given below.

The Dhebar Commission in (1961) recommended an integrated approach based on the minimum essential items like food, drinking water, employment, education, health services and village roads.

In 1972 the task force on development of tribal areas suggested that the ecological, occupational and social preemptors of the tribal population must be properly assessed for formulation of a policy and its implementation so that a flow of benefits could be assured to the tribal people.

The Dupe Committee in 1972 tried to define a new strategy for tribal development and suggested the problem of tribal development. The committee defined tribal problem at the national level and suggested an integrated area development approach in national level for tribal development.

3.3 Tribal Development Through the Five Year Plans

The special programme for tribal development has been implemented by Government of India for the benefit of tribal population.

3.3.1 First Five Year Plan (1951-56)

In the first Five Year Plan, the Government of India laid the foundation stone for tribal development. The main objective was to bring about the overall change of the tribes and tribal areas through Community Development Programmes (CDP). The tribals are adapting modernization without sacrificing their own culture. The development programmes of the State for tribal were broadly divided into four heads, viz. (a) Education and culture, (b) Development of Tribal Economy, (c) Communication and (d) Social Welfare like health, sanitation, housing etc.

During this Plan, expenditure on tribals was 17.47 crores out of the total expenditure of Rs.1960 crores. While the tribal population was 2.25 crores, the expenditure on the development of tribals was only 0.83%.

3.3.2 Second Five Year Plan (1956-61)

During this time the Government of India initiated a massive programme of integrated development through the National Extension Blocks (NEB) in tribal areas. Each area covering an average population of 25,000 that block known as Special Multipurpose Tribal Development Block (SMPT) and nodal administration system was introduced. This programme covered nearly 71 per cent of tribal areas in throughout the country.

As per the recommendation of V.Elwin Committee, SMPT Blocks were reorganized and renamed as Tribal Development Blocks (TDB). Each TDB was allowed to cover 25,000 tribals as against 65,000 in normal blocks and the geographical area.

3.3.3 Third Five Year Plan (1961-66)

In this Plan, various programmes were drawn up and were considered by the special working group in the signal of the economic uplifment. It has recommended formation of multi-purpose cooperatives to meet their credit and non-credit need of the agricultural and artisans. This programmes aimed improvement of land, land reclamation, social conservation, minor irrigation, subsidiary cost of improved seeds and manure, bullocks, provision of training facilities and demonstration, fisheries, poultry, sheep rearing and breeding, organization of training cum production centers.

In this Plan period education was given priority in tribal areas and providing stipends, scholarships and fellowship also. At the same time medical and health care programme for maternity and chilled welfare centers were aslo created.

During this period the special committee was appointed by the Home Ministry. The committee recommended additional blocks. The Committee has not only confined to scheduled areas but non-scheduled areas, also where ST concentration is more than 55 per cent. The committee recommended for opening 480 blocks during this period. The total expenditure on the tribal during this Plan was of the order of Rs. 52.55 crores out of a total of Rs. 8577 crores.

In this Plan period, the top priority was given to the economic upliftment of tribals followed by education, health, housing and communication for the tribal.

3.3.4 Fourth Five Year Plan (1969-74)

In this Plan period 489 Tribal Development block (TD) had come in to existences for the betterment of the scheduled tribe. The Shilu A. O Committee reviewed the working of T.D. block in the country. It evaluated its success and made the observations.

1. The Performance of T.D. Blocks fell short of expectations.
2. Employment generation was narrow.
3. Schemes were tailored to suit the local people.
4. Development benefits were confined to the upper class tribal communities.

In this Plan period six projects were introduced in the tribal areas covering around 40,000 tribal families with an investment of Rs. 150 cores per projects. These project were known as Tribal Development Agencies (TDA) and were taken up in the sector. This Agency adopts mostly agricultural, veterinary services and fisheries as the core of economic sectors.

During the Plan, the criteria of covering Community Development Block (CD) to Tribal Development Block (TD) have changed the name. In 1961, if a C.D. Block has 50 per cent of scheduled tribe population, it could qualify for conversion of tribal development block. The state government suggested to National Government for conversion of 47 C.D. Blacks to T.D. Block during this period.

The Government implemented most important programme to raise the economic condition of tribal through the Tribal Development Block Programme. Beside, the development schemes are education, economic upliftment, health and housing etc. The incomplete and schematic approach of T.D. Blocks and backward class welfare programmes were not found quite successful. In the end of the Plan period six Tribal Development agencies were started throughout the country and two were started during the Fifth Plan.

3.3.5 Fifth Five Year Plan (1974-79)

During the Plan period to eradicate the weakness of the earlier area based programmes, viz. Tribal Development Blocks and Tribal Development Agencies, a new strategy was evolved in this Plan period and foundation of Tribal Sub-Plan for the tribal areas.

The tribal problems are classified in two categories (a) Area of Tribal concentration and (b) Dispersed Tribes.

During the Plan period an important landmark was the development of tribal areas with the objects of doubling the income of state at current price for meeting the minimum consumption needs of the people and removal of imbalances.

The concept of Sub-Plan is an area development approach which is planned to provide to the special needs of the tribal and integrate the area approach strategy. It put much emphasis on all round development of tribal. The main intentions of the Sub-Plan were

(a) To improve the qulity of life of tribal communities

(b) To narrow down the gap between the level of development of tribal and other-areas.

(c) To achieve social and cultural integration of tribals with the rest of the society.

The Planning Commission setup a Task-Force during Fifth Five Year Plan to Review the development of tribal areas. A new strategy was issued for planning and development of the tribal areas through the Sub-Plan. The main object was to eliminate all forms of exploitation, accelerating process of socio-economic changes.

The Plan covered around 65 per cent of the total tribal population of the country. The highest priority was given to elimination of exploitation of tribes as a first step for economic upliftment. Based on the guidelines of the Sub-Plan approach integrated tribal development programmes (ITDPs) were introduced.

The tribal Sub-Plan covered all scheduled areas and more than 50 per cent tribal population. The substantial tribal population was covered under the plan, according to these formulations. Bihar 72 per cent, Orissa 68 per cent, Himachal Pradesh 9 per cent, Gujarat 59 per cent, Madhya Pradesh 75 per cent, Manipur 94 per cent, Goa, Diu, Daman 100 per cent, Nagaland and Nagar Haweli 99 per cent, Rajasthan 44 per cent. This was relaxed for reasonable proportion of tribal population states, like Andhra Pradesh, Karnataka, Kerala, Tamil Nadu, West Bengal and Uttar Pradesh. In the Plan were covered 16 states and 2 Union Territories.

It was observed that the Sub-Plan approach had limited success, due to the administrative inadequacies, lack of managerial skill and lack of proper monitoring and evaluations. The most of tribal areas are inaccessible with scattered habitations; gain from various schemes could not reach the tribal areas.

3.3.6 Sixth Five Year Plan (1980-85)

At the end Fourth Plan covered only 40 per cent of the tribal population of the country. But due to the implementation of various Sub-Plan programmes during the Fifth Plan, was increased 65 per cent of total tribal population. There was no special attention given to the problems of the remaining 35 per cent of dispersed tribal groups. The Government of India realized that the tribals are living in isolated and inaccessible areas and they are hardly benefited from general development.

During the Sixth Plan, the Government considered areas of tribal population hither to not covered within the orbit of the tribal Sub-Plan. The areas with 50 per cent of concentration of tribal were brought within the Sub-Plan, with an intention to cover 75 per cent of total tribal areas.

The main objective of the Plan was to bring all the tribal population under suitable development programmes, to reduce the gap between the tribal areas and the surrounding areas by the end of Sixth Plan.

During the Plan period two important approaches were launched viz.

(1) Modified Area Development Approach (MADA) and

(2) Community Development Approach (CDA).

For primitive tribal special income generating schemes were introduced during the Plan.

The development approach of this Plan was divided into four major parts, for the integration of services at the delivery point of the beneficiary with a view to cultivate self reliance.

(a) Development of services from the bottom upwards instead of top downwards.

(b) Development of skills to diversify the occupation.

(c) Introduction of modern technology based on local materials and local skills to remove social stigma attached to their present profession.

(d) Further the Plan proposed to reform garnets and subsidy system so that the beneficiary becomes self-reliant over a specified period.

3.3.7 Seventh Five Year Plan (1985-90)

In this Plan period the principal object was social justice, equity, self-reliance, improved efficiency and productivity of tribal areas. During this Plan period there was more concentration on social justice, employment and poverty reduction.

The Tribal Sub-Plan already covered 75 per cent of tribal population during the Sixth Five Year Plan. The programmes for tribal concentration pockets are tribal concentration pockets are already identified and Plans for the 72 primitive tribal groups were to be formulated and executed.

The Seventh Plan was based on beneficiary oriented infrastructure, and human resources human development programmes. The overall objective was providing assistance to 50 per cent ST families.

This Plan mainly focused on the remaining to be introduced mix of area-com-family development. Simultaneously paying attention to the vulnerable sector amongst the Scheduled Tribes it can easily be ascertained. In the period around 40 lakhs STs Families below the poverty line are together to be provided economic assistances to eradicate the poverty.

During the plan period, 3 new ITDPs have been added in Sikkim, by STs Population concentration norms as a special case and by the end of 1987-88, the total of 184 ITDPs were functioning. The ITDPs area covered around 313.21 lakhs tribal population in this period.

During the period the appropriate guidelines were introduced in favor of the states, to undertake the followings for the tribal areas

(a) Cabinet sub-committee was formed to decide broad objectives of the tribal sub-plan

(b) Tribal representatives were associated with plan implementation,

(c) ITDPs should be given full control,

(d) Prohibition of transfer of tribal lands to non-tribals and

(e) Dedicated services of the officers.

In the Plan period, introduced intermediary formula between agriculture and shifting cultivation was also thought the tribal areas to restore ecology. A policy for the rehabilitation of displaced tribals of development project areas was undertaken during the plan period.

For the economic development of SCs and Scheduled Tribes, two national level institutions were set up viz.

(I) Tribal Cooperative Marketing Development Federation (TRIFED) in 1987 as an apex body for State Tribal Development Cooperative Corporations; and

(ii) National Scheduled Castes and Scheduled Tribes Finance and Development Corporation (NSFDC) in 1989. The former was envisaged to provide remunerative price for the Forest and Agriculture Produce of tribal, while the latter was intended to provide credit support for employment generation.

3.3.8 Eighth Five year Plan (1992-97)

In this plan period vigorous programmes and schemes for tribal areas were brought in for the removal of development bottlenecks, elimination of exploitation, oppression, suppression of money-lending businessmen, non-payment of minimum wages and right to collect minor forest produce (MFP) etc.

A primary objective of tribal poverty, illiteracy, ignorance and exploitations is considered through special component plan, TSP and other special schemes. Co-operatives are designed to render services in the tribal areas mainly marketing for SAP and MFP.

During the period various schemes are introduced like, watershed projects, agricultural, social forestry, horticulture, infrastructure and social services, etc.

3.3.9 Ninth Five Year Plan (1997-2002)

During the plan period, the main objective was to strengthen and bridge the gap between the scheduled tribes and rest of the population. Thorough the literacy states is one of the main indicators of socioeconomic development, and employment opportunities largely depend on the level of education. However, the purpose was to strengthen the infrastructure facilities like construction of schools buildings, additional classrooms, laboratory building, provision of lab equipment, computers, furniture and play martial, up gradation of schools, at all levels, opening of residential schools, construction of vocational training centers, providing basic amenities like toilets, drinking water etc.

The National Common Minimum Programme was launched for evaluating minor irrigation for adivasi and dalits. The minor irrigation schemes for land owned by tribes under the assistance provided to states for bridging infrastructure help in tribal areas under the Article 275 (1) of the constitution of India.

After implementing the TSPs Plan in 1974 in the fifth five year plan till the end of the ninth plan, the SCA to TSPs was intended for filling up the critical gaps in family based income generating activities through the TSPs

The main objective was providing education to the tribal students. During the Plan period, Ekalavaya Model Residential Schools was introduced in the year of 1997-98 under the Article 275 (1) constitution, all over India setting 100 model residential schools from the class VI to XII for getting higher education and getting higher level jobs in the Governmental and various public sector services.

Approach adopted for Scheduled Tribe

(1) Efforts were made to ensure that the tribal economy is protected and supported against threats from the external markets. The ownership/patent Rights of the tribal people in respect of minor forest produce vis-à-vis the use of medicinal plants will be protected as per the provisions of Intellectual Property Rights (IPR).

(2) The Primitive Tribal Groups are leading an extremely precarious existence and some of them are on the verge of extinction. Existing

development programmes have not been able to alleviate their condition. An Action Plan incorporating total food and nutritition security, health coverage, education facilities etc. in keeping with their socio-cultural conditions will be prepared by the Central/State Governments. The proposed Action Plan will have in-built flexibility to cater to the specific needs of each such tribe and its environment.

(3) A National policy for tribal development will be formulated at the earliest.

The percentage of the tribal population in poverty has continued to decline, even if not as much as was targeted. Literacy has increased from 52% in 1991 to 65% in 2001 and the improvement is evident in all states (Hasnain 2007).

3.3.10 Tenth Five Year Plan (2002-2007)

During the Plan period, the objective was to reduce vulnerability, land alienation, indebtedness, rehabilitation and various issues. A comprehensive National Policy for Empowering Tribal development in the Tenth Five Year Plan was formulated.

One of the objectives of this plan was increasing the economic growth for national planning over the years of tribal development. The objective was increasing the GDP per capita income but broader enhancement of human well being. Increasing adequate level of consumption of food and other types of consumption goods and also access basic social services particularly education, health, and availability of drinking water, sanitation and expansion of economic and social opportunities for all tribal over the country.

3.3.10.1 Education Programmes

The scheme for construction of hostels for girls and boys, separate schemes for the construction of hostels for scheduled tribe boys launched in 1989-90. The primary objectives of the scheme promote literacy among the tribal students. To providing hostel and accommodation, for poor economic conditions of tribal students for not able to continue their education. The schemes provide for the hostel as well as for extension of exiting hostels building for middle schools, secondary school and college and university level education.

3.3.10.2 Women Empowerment

The tribal women are at educationally low level in all over India. This Plan, identified 134 districts are below 10 per cent of literacy thought the country.

National Scheduled Tribe Finances Development Corporation introduced an exclusive scheme for economic development tribal women beneficiaries, entitled on "Adivasi Mahila Sashatikaran Yojana" (AMSY) for providing concessional financial assistance (Gov.India).

The ministry decided to provide insurances cover to the earning members of each PTG families throughout the country under the 'Janasri Bheema Yojana' of Life Insurances Corporation of India.

3.3.11 Eleventh Five Year Plan (2007-2012)

The Eleventh Plan period was inclusive growth approach identical with social justice as it primarily addresses, the tribal issues of exclusion, exploitation, marginalization, unrest and government concerning tribals and tribal areas.

The social empowerment, particularly in educational development recognising that educational development as an basic social empowerment, various schemes extending incentives, financial assistance, coaching and hostel facilities are being implemented for the benefit of STs.

The economic empowerment through the employment and income-generating activities, livelihood and social justice through prevention of exploitation, land alienation, involuntary displacement and survival protection and development of endangered PTGs.

This Plan period has focused on the following four activities, namely

(1) Retail marketing development activity

(2) Minor forest produces marketing development activity

(3) Vocation training, skill up gradation and a capacity building of ST artisans and MFP gatherers, and

(4) Research and development, intellectual property right, IPR proper activity

The total SCA released to States/UTs under TSP in the Eleventh Plan was in the order of Rs. 2,872.10 crore. About 15 lakh STs were assisted to cross the poverty line during the Eleventh Plan.

3.3.12 Twelfth Five Year Plan (2012-2017)

The prime object of the 12th Five Year Plan, through the Tribal Sub Plan is development of tribal areas. The TSP has set the twin objectives: (*i*) socioeconomic development of STs; and (*ii*) protection of tribals against exploitation of others. Through realisation of these objectives, the ultimate aim of the TSP strategy is to narrow down for the development gap in tribals population and rest of the population.

The development of tribal economy under TSP is envisaged through sectoral efforts as given below.

(I) Agriculture and allied activities, through provision of minor and medium irrigation facilities supplemented by programmes for animal husbandry, dairying, poultry etc.

(II) Improvised credit and marketing facilities so as to ensure adequate return of the produce of the tribals in respect of agriculture and minor forest products.

(III) Special training programmes for tribal farmers for agricultural extension supported by the provision of agricultural infrastructure.

(IV) Preparing suitable forestry programmes ensuring tribals' participation as equal partners

(V) Promoting agricultural production through improved method of cultivation and rural electrification to promote small scale industry.

(VI) Reorganizing basic services such as nutritional interventions, education, health services, public distribution system, employment generating activities under MGNREGA with posting adequate staff with surety of tenure and assurance of funds to implement these programmes.

(VII) The emphasis on education, health and livelihood support for tribal.

(VIII) Better coverage of roadways for tribal areas (population of 500-1,000), with population up to 100 being covered in LWE (Left Wing Extremism) to be connected.

(IX) Land acquisition of tribal land to be addressed as required under PESA and displaced tribal population to be resettled and rehabilitated.

(X) Increase coverage of the most vulnerable within the Scheduled Tribes in the health sector. Increase cadre of health workers to better serve tribal.

Those are the objectives to ensure the socioeconomic condition, education, health and livelihood opportunities etc.

3.4 Government of Tamil Nadu programmes for the welfare of Adi Dravidar and Tribal population.

- Abolition of Bonded Labour System
- Adi Dravidar and Tribal Welfare Department -Hostels - Special Guides
- Adi Dravidar and Tribal Welfare Department -Incentive / Award of Prizes - District Level Prize plus2 Examination Rs.3000/- 10th Std First prize Rs.1000/- Second Prize Rs.500/- Third Prize Rs.300/.
- Adi Dravidar and Tribal Welfare Department -Incentive / Award of Prizes - For each subjects (c) plus2 Examination Rs.2000/- (d)10th Std Examination Rs.1000/-
- Adi Dravidar and Tribal Welfare Department -Scholarship - Free Education upto 12th Std. to all i.e. tuition fee will not be collected and the amount will be reimbursed by Government.
- Adi Dravidar and Tribal Welfare Department -Scholarship - Public Examination fee for 10th and 12th Std.
- Adi Dravidar and Tribal Welfare Department - Stationary - Text Books
- Admission of Adi Dravidar / Tribal students in plus-one at reputed schools.
- Afforestation schemes providing incentives and providing employment to Tribals in Forest Operation.

- All India Service Examinations like I.A.S., I.P.S., I.R.S., etc.
- Animal Husbandry
- Annal Gandhi Memorial Award
- Annal Gandhi Memorial Award - Two (One Boy and One Girl) Hindu AD Students in each district who have secured first rank in the 12th Std Public Examinations and continue their studies.
- Assistance for Funeral Rites
- Assistance to Lawyers for Starting their Practice
- Award of Rs.20,000/- to Best Writers
- Awards to Bright Students
- Book Bank - Books will be purchased for Medical/ Engineering/ Law / M.B.A./Veterinary / Agri. and Polytechnic / courses and placed in the Library.
- Burial Ground - Provision of Burial Grounds and pathway to Burial Grounds
- Chief Minister Merit Award- Given Rs.3000/- per annum for 5 years
- Chief Minister s Merit Award
- Community Halls
- Construction of free houses for tribals
- Development of Agricultural lands
- District Collector s Discretionary Fund
- District Level award for XII std
- District Level award for X std
- Dr. Ambedkar National merit Scholarship
- Drinking Water facility - Provision of drinking water facilities to AD and Tribal Habitations
- Employment opportunities to Educated Tribal Youths
- Exemption of Examination Fees / Application Fees / Registration Fees
- Exemption of Special fees and Examination Fees to the Post Graduate Girl students.
- Exemption of Special Fees and Examination Fees to the Under Graduate students
- Exemption of Tuition Fees

- Free Education - Granting of admission fees, Registration fees to ADs / Tribals / AD Converted to Christianity Girls students who join Degree, Post Graduate Degree, Professional Courses
- Free Education - Special fee and Examination fee to students studying in B.A., B.Sc., B.Com, other degree courses and Girl Students of P.G. Courses.
- Free Education - Special fee and Examination fee to students studying in B.A., B.Sc., B.Com, other degree courses and Girl Students of P.G. Courses. Special fee and Examination fee to students study
- Government of India Post-Metric Scholarship Scheme
- Government of India Pre-Metric Scholarship Scheme for the children of those engaged in unclean occupation
- Grant of States Overseas Scholarship - Scholarship to AD/Tribal students pursuing higher studies in abroad.
- Higher Education Special Scholarship
- Higher Education Special Scholarship Scheme
- Hill area development programme.
- Hostels - Free Boarding and lodging to student studying up to 12th standard
- Hostels - mats and bed sheets
- Hostels - Uniforms
- Housing and other schemes (house sites are provided at free of cost 3 cents in rural, 1 ½ cents in municipal area and 1 cent in corporation areas AD/ Tribal families who do not own house or house site. The annual income ceiling Rs. 16,000 in rural and Rs.24,000 in urban areas)
- Housing and other Schemes - Encroachments will be regularized for issue of pattas
- Housing Scheme (do not own a house to provide house site Ptta)
- Incentive / award of prizes - state level (a) plus2 public examination Rs. 25,000/-(b)10th public examination Rs. 10,000/-
- Individual entrepreneur development scheme
- Insurance scheme to the primitive tribal (janasree beema yojana scheme)

- Issue of tools and appliances - sewing machines/carpentry things. (iron boxes will be supplied to those who undertook ironing as a trade)
- Job Oriented Training - 2.2 Typewriting and shorthand
- Land Development Scheme
- Land Purchase Scheme
- Link road - link roads are provided connecting the ad/tribal habitation with the main roads / villages
- Maintenance Charges - Dayscholars
- Maintenance charges - hostellers
- Merit-cum-Means Award
- Merit cum means award - conditions and prize amounts for grant of this award are as per the Gandhi memorial award. This award is meant for tirbals and adi dravidar converted to Christianity.
- Note Books
- National Safai Karamcharis Finance and Development Corporation (NSKFDC) (Individual maximum unit cost Rs.5.00 lakhs, subsidy 30 percent of the unit cost subject to a maximum of Rs.25,000/- balance amount (Term Loan) provided by TAHDCO at nominal rate of interest)
- NSLRS (National Scheme for Liberation and Rehabilitation of Scavengers) (Individual loan maximum Unit cost Rs.50,000/- subsidy 50 percent of the unit cost subject to maximum of Rs.10,000/- margin money 15 percent unit cost maximum of Rs.7500/- and balance Bank LoanRs.32,500)
- Overseas Scholarship
- Post metric Scholarship - All compulsorily payable fees, Exam fees and maintenance charges payable to Schools and Colleges are sanctioned as scholarship.
- Providing interest free loan to tribals, provision of essential articles at reasonable price and marketing the minor forest products to ensure better returns to the tribals through lamp societies.
- Provision of link road facilities to the tribal village connecting with plains or main villages

- Provision of Minor Irrigation
- Provision of street lights to Tribal habitations.
- Schemes of Tribal Welfare Department
- Scholarship - Assistance to the children of those engaged in unclean occupations
- Scholarship - beyond 12th std. students studying in govt. / govt. aided institutions are exempted from payment of tuition fees. the amount will be reimbursed to the head of the institution by govt.
- Scholarship - Granting of Special fee
- Sericulture scheme
- Special Assistance to Law Graduates
- Special Fee concession
- Special Incentive Scheme for encouraging girls education
- Special incentives to girl students
- Special Prize Money Award - Grant of one time award to the Graduates and Post Graduate and Professional courses.
- Special Prize Money scheme
- State Government's Special Post-Metric Scholarship (beyond X Std.)
- State level Toppers Award
- State level Toppers award for X Standard
- Subamathi Self Help Group
- Subject toppers award (25 Subjects)
- Subject toppers award (5 Subjects)
- Supply of 10 Beehives at free of cost for collecting honey
- Training in basket making, tailoring etc. for the women
- Vocational Guidance center are functioning at Udhagamandalam to the guidance of Tribal youths for employment purpose
- Vocational Training Programme (Govt. of Tamil Nadu, 2018)

References:

Government of Tamil Nadu (2018) Adi Dravidar and Tribal welfare Department, http://www.tn.gov.in/scheme/department_wise/1.

Chapter IV

Profile of The Study Area

4.1 Introduction

Profile of the study area is given here to know the existing socio-economic condition of the study area. This chapter has been divided into three parts, namely, (a) Profile of Thiruvannamalai district, (b) Profile of Jawadhu Hills and (c) Profile of Sample Village, Puliyur.

4.2 Thiruvannamalai District

Thiruvannamalai district came into existence on 30th September 1989. It was carved in from North Arcot district. The total geographical area of Thiruvannamalai district is 6,188 Sq. Km. There are two revenue divisions in this district. They are Thiruvannamalai and Cheyyar. This district has eight taluks. They are: Thiruvannamalai, Chengam, Thandrampattu, Polur, Arni, Cheyyar, Kalasapakkam and Vandavasi. There are 18 Blocks, four municipalities, ten Panchayats unions. The district is bounded on the North and West by Vellore district and on the South West by Dharmapuri district on the South Villupuram district and on the East by Kancheepuram district.

4.2.1 Total Population of the District

Thiruvannamalai district is at 13th place in terms of population in the state. The total population of the district is 24.65 lakhs; 13.35 lakhs male 12.30 female, as per 2011 census. The urban population is 4.95 lakhs and rural population is 19.70 lakhs. The density of population is around 473 per Sq. Km. The ST population is 4.27 per cent of the total population. This is 23 per cent for SC. The sex ratio is 994 female for 1000 male population. The total literacy rate is74 per cent in the district.

4.2.2 Forest and hills areas

The area under Reserve Forest is 1, 06,653 hectares and it is concentrated in Chengam and Polur Taluks. The important forest produces are Sandalwood, Eucalyptus, Bamboo etc. The important hills in the district are Jawadhu Hills (2,500 feet above the sea level), Kailasagiri (2,743 feet above the sea level) and Thiruvannalamai (2,608 feet above the sea level). One sixth of the area of this district is covered by reserve forest and hill which is part and parcel of Eastern Ghats under Jawadhu Hills.

4.2.3 Profile of Jawadhu Hills

Jawadhu Hills is located in the Thiruvannamalai District of Tamil Nadu State. Jawadhu Hills has a height of 4,000 meters and a maximum spared around 40 Sq.km. It is a part of the Eastern Ghats of India. The centre and south of Jawadhu Hills extensive undulating plateau with large valleys ranging between 500 meters and 800 meters. Kambhangudi Malai is the highest peak in Jawadhu Hills having more than 300 feet height. Jawadhu Hills consists of steep rocky and precipitate soils. The climate is favorable to the growth of sandalwood trees. The total population of Jawadhu Hills is over 47,081 as per the 2011 census of India.

4.2.4 Malaiyali Tribe

Mala means Hills and yalee means rules who rule the Jawadhu Hills. It is one of the tribe communities in India and they are living for several decades in this hills area. This society is spread across the mountains of Jawadhu Hills which is shared by the judiciary of two districts namely Vellore and Thiruvannamalai. The major share of this community is in Thiruvannamalai district and little share is retained under Vellore district. Evidence at Keel Cheppli stone houses proves that existence of human civilization has a history of over 5,000 years. The human population of the Jamunmadthur block is around one lakh. Out of which 98 per cent are from tribal community and 2% are from other communities. This hill is around 3,000 feet above the sea level. This Jawadhu Hills is popular for its Sandalwood, Teakwood and Rosewood and different herbal species.

Elephants, foxes, deers, forest buffalo and monkeys are spotted in the mountain ranges.

4.2.5 Social system

Early marriage is common here: 15 to 18 years for boys and 13 to 18 years for girls Premarital sex, escape, extra marital sex are commonly accepted in this tribal area. Around 70% tribal are illiterate. The religion is Hindu and any conversion is strictly prohibited. If anybody is converted to other religion, he / she will be immediately excommunicated. People will not go to those houses even for births and deaths.

4.2.6 Education

The Jawadhu hills total literacy rate in 2011was 42 per cent. Compared to district level (73.36 per cent) this is very low. The male and female literacy rates were 50.07 and 32.86 per cent respectively. The gender gap in literacy was notified as 17.21 per cent. In school enrollment in primary level 100 per cent in the area, but the gross enrollment of the secondary level is 59.93 per cent in this hills. The tribal children have to walk for around 5 km to reach school. Because of this, school enrollment for primary level is 99.40 per cent. At the same time, drop-out was high in upper primary level (24.87 per cent) (EER 2013 & DISE). Very few children are going to school beyond 8th standard. Female education is neglected in this area because most of the girls children attaining puberty in the age of 12-14 years immediately getting married. So, female drop-out was very high in the area. Even few people who are literate are unemployed in this hill. So others get de-motivated.

The system of education in these areas is very poor. Out of total enrolment, the dropout rate is alarmingly touching 60 percent after middle schooling due to unorganized education system, inadequate infrastructure of the schools, irregularity of the teachers in the classroom and schools, non-involvement of the parents etc. This has led to high percent of dropouts at school level. Last two year's percentage of pass in higher secondary school at Jawadhu hills is low and quality of education is declining. There are 35 Primary schools, 18 middle schools, 2 high schools and 3 higher secondary schools in Jawadhu Hills as per education department (DISE 2016).

4.2.7 Economic problems

Around 80% of the tribal people are living BPL. Agriculture is their major occupation. Rain water cultivation is possible. There is no check dam and non-availability of water is a major problem during summer. The land scape is not suitable to harvest rain water. So, for six months they stay in a tribal area and for other six months they migrate to Kerala, Karnataka and Andhra Pradesh for their livelihood. Because of their migration, the families are disintegrated. The per capita income of the district, which was Rs. 24,711 in 2005-06, has increased to Rs 41,569 in 2012 (Go.TN 2012). The tribal per capita income was less. More than 80% of the adults are liquor addicts and exhaust all money on the consumption of liquor. This is one of the attributing factors of tribal poverty.

In Jawadhu Hills employment opportunities are generated through MGNREGA. It can be seen that the district administration and local Panchayat institutions could not identify required work. In the Jawadhu Hills 44 per cent of the households engage in the job.

The highest number of child labourers is found in Jawadhu Hills. About 49 percent of the male and 46 percent of the female children work as child labour in Jawadhu Hills (Tiruvannamalai District Human Development Report 2017).

4.2.8 Health problems

More than 70 per cent of the adult men and women have venereal diseases. Reproductive tract infection is one of the major health problems for women. In Jawadhu Hills the prevalence of anemia among adolescent girls was 95.5 percent and 45.4 percent of children less than three years are malnourished (Thiruvannamalai District Human Development Report 2017). Infant mortality rate and maternal mortality rate are around 5 times higher than the national average. The traditional healers are playing an important role. Their health seeking behaviours and health practices are harmful. Government has acknowledged this health problem and started some health project. But it failed due to non-availability of qualified doctors in primary health centres. Almost 100% women are anemic. Anemia among pregnant women and home delivery are the major reasons for the higher mortality of infants and mothers. Jawadhu Hills. According to the Palamarathur study in Jawadhu Hills, 6.79 percent of the adolescent girls only fall on normal HB level. The rest of them are anemic. NRHM's programme of anemia control and reduction was implemented in Jawadhu hills and DHAN Foundation was part of the programme. 50,000 adolescents and 12,000 pregnant women were covered (ibid, 2017).

4.3 Profile of Jawadhu Hills

There are 272 hamlets in Jawadhu Hills, located is Polur taluk. The people in Jawadhu Hills are brown as Malayalis. However they themselves call as Vellalar and Saanars.

4.3.1 Profile of Sample village Puliyur

Puliyur village located in Southern part of Jawadhu Hills. This village is located in the main road between Jaminamdhur and Chengam. This is the main village which consists of a few hamlets namely Killthadiyapattu, Mallthadiyapattu, Erukkampattu, Nellivai and Thalur.

The size of population of Puliyur hamlet is 478 and literacy rate is just 43 per cent as per 2011 census. Killthadiyapattu has 78 persons as per 2011 census. These persons have come to this hamlet from Kangipuram and Thiruvallu districts of Tamil Nadu. Every house in this hamlet has got electricity connection and avail the provisions distributed by the Public Distribution System (PDS). There are 54 households in Mellthadiyapattu hamlet. This hamlet has got well and cannel irrigation facilities. Some fruit varieties are cultivated. Traders frequently visit this hamlet for the purchase of fruits. Erukkampattu hamlet consists of 58 households. Compared to other hamlets, this hamlet has got slightly larger cattle population. Each household has got around 15 cattle. There are 109 households in Nellivoy hamlet. Pucca road facility is available for Thalur hamlet. Hence the people of this hamlet take up jobs outside the hamlet too.

The Puliyur revenue village has got 100 per cent drinking water and electricity connections. There is a Village Administrative Officer, sub primary health center, ICDS (integrated child development schemes) Anganvadi maiyam, forest residential middle school, the central government middle school (KGBVRS) for drop-out girls, panchayath office, two buildings for self help groups (SHGs) of women, post office, village library, two PDS centers, two panchayath commercial places and etc.

Table 4.1 District Panchayat Union population and Scheduled Tribe (STs) population.

Si. No	Panchayat Union	No. of Villages	Total Population in lakhs	Total STs in (000)	Percentage
1	Tiruvannamalai	69	1.89	3.78	2.10
2	Keelapennathur	45	1.04	2.47	2.37
3	Thurinjapuram	47	1.23	1.66	1.34
4	Polur	40	1.35	0.47	0.35
5	Chetpet	49	0.94	0.36	0.38
6	**Jawadhu Hills**	**11**	**0.51**	**47.1**	**90.54**
7	Kalasapakkam	45	1.21	0.44	0.36
8	Chengam	44	1.42	2.45	1.72
9	Pudupalayam	37	0.89	1.12	1.24
10	Thandrampet	47	1.78	17.10	9.52
11	Cheyyar	53	0.94	1.13	1.20
12	Anakkavur	55	.078	1.28	1.63
13	Vembakkam	64	1.27	1.35	1.05
14	Vandavasi	61	1.11	2.20	1.95
15	Thellar	61	0.97	2.23	2.27
16	Peranamallur	57	0.85	1.14	1.33
17	Arani	38	1.16	0.52	0.44
18	West Arani	37	1.10	0.38	0.34
Total Thiruvannamalai District		860	20.39	87.15	4.27

Sources: Census of India 2011.

Table 4.2 Total population of Jawadhu Hills by Panchayats-wise

Si.No	Name of the Panchayat	Total Population	Total STs	Percentage of ST population
1	Atipattu	1,070	1,068	99.81
2	Kallathur	2,623	1,613	61.49
3	Kanamalai	6,666	5,983	89.75
4	Kovilur	12,753	11,006	86.30
5	Kuttakarai	3,560	3,242	91.06
6	Melcilambadi	3,882	3,785	97.50
7	Nammiyampattu	8,222	7,569	92.05
8	Palamaruthur	3,486	3,305	94.80
9	**Puliyur**	**1,690**	**1,665**	**98.52**
10	Urgoundanur	1,988	1,911	96.12
11	Veerappanur	6,061	5,934	97.90
Total		51,999	47,081	90.54

Sources: Census of India 2011.

Table 4.3. Total population of sample village by hamlets

Si. No	Name of the village	Total population	Total number of households
1	Erukambattu	248	58
2	Kilthattiyapattu	78	19
3	Melthattiyapattu	240	54
4	Nellivoy	410	109
5	Perumuttam	247	66
6	Puliyur	467	113
	Grand Total	1690	419

Source: Census of India 2011.

Table 4.4 Puliyur Village Panchayath Information

Si. No	Item	No.
1	Total population	1690
2	Total wards	6
3	Panchayath buildings	1
4	Total hamlets	6
5	Post offices	1
6	PDS building	2
7	Anganwadi centers	7
8	Schools 1. Primary school-1 2. Meddle school & with building (Monitor by TN forest department)-1 3. KGBVRS-1	3
9	Hospital	1
10	Village Library	1
11	Self help group building	1
12	Women public toilet	1
13	Panchayath Commercial building	3

Source: Village Panchayath information board.

Chapter V

Differences Between the Households Living BPL and APL

5.1 Introduction

For the purpose of the study the total sample households (113) have been grouped into two.

1. The households living BPL and
2. The households living APL.

Poverty line is defined as income of Rs.50 per capita per day. If the households have a per capita per day income of less than Rs. 50, they have been brought under BPL. Other households living with more than Rs.50 per day per capita income are considered as living APL. According to this definition 70 per cent of the sampled households (76) are living BPL (BPLHs) and only 30 per cent of the sampled households (37) are living APL (APLHs.)

5.2 Differences Between the Households living BPL and APL.

5.2.1 Nature of Families

There is no significant difference between them in terms of the nature of family. In both groups, the proportion of nuclear families is slightly more than the proportion of joint families (vide Table 5.1). Hence the nature of family does not seem to explain their economic status.

Average family size is larger in BPLHs (4.5 members) than in APLHs (3.5 members). Those may be the reason for lower per capita income in BPLHs.

5.3.2 Education

Generally, poor transport facilities and roads is the main reason for low literacy. There are only three bus trips provided by government. Private mini buses come to Puliyur only twice a day. There are two schools. First, the Forest Residential School is taken for discussion. The roofed area of the school is 2,200 sq.ft. There are 140 students – 40 per cent girls and 60 per cent of boys are studying. There are eight teachers. Three teachers' salary is paid by the government of Tamil Nadu and remaining five teachers are paid by one Non-Governmental Organization. Student in this school study upto 8th standard, after that they have to go to some other schools. At this stage there is larger dropouts. All girls in this school get scholarships of Rs. 500 per annum. Drinking water facility is there. Toilets are not in usable condition. Hence the students do not use toilets.

The other school namely KGPVRS (Kasturba Gandhi Balika Vidyalaya Residential School), is run by central government. There are eight teachers and 80 students. All the eight teachers' salary is paid by central government. The girls only are allowed. The girls are in one way or the other are from disadvantaged section. They are orphans, child workers, poor performers' etc., Drinking water and toilets are available. However , the students prefer open defecations.

There are some differences in terms of illiteracy among the two groups of households. More than 70 per cent of the respondents of BPLHs (BPLRs) are illiterate. This percentage is only 54 for the respondents of APLHs (APLRs). With university degree, it could be believed that some of the APLHs could get better earning jobs and hence their economic status may be slightly better than that of the BPLRs. However, in the study area it has not happened! There is no significant difference in the employment status between the BPLRs and APLRs (Vide Table 5.2). Therefore it is the economic status which has influenced the educational status, not vice versa. The students of this village, like others, get university degrees, but they are unable to get better job. Either the students' skills levels are very low or employment opportunities are very limited or both. It is difficult to make any conclusive statement here. But looking at the macro level data, it is gradually losing its significance in terms of improving the skills of the students.

The previews study results show that tribal children drop-out was very high in the school education in particularly after completing the middle or secondary level of education (Amulya Kumar Benerat, 2015).

The Malayali tribal community have very low level of literacy compared to the general population and wide range of inequality (Jayakumar and Planiyammal, 2016).

5.2.3 Employment

The major sources of employment are agriculture, For women workers the wage rate is around Rs.100 per day. Men prefer migration to other states, particularly Kerala and Andhra Pradesh, where salaries are three times higher. In villages they engage in some agricultural works, where they are paid Rs.2,000 per day. They go to Andhra Pradesh mostly for wood cutting works. In Kerala they take up construction activities. In Cheyyar, Coimmbatore and Tiruppur spinning mills provide jobs for some girls. Mostly they stay there for about three months, and the remaining nine months they do some agricultural work. MGNREGS also provides substantial employment opportunities. They also collect forest products and sell in the market for making money.

As stated earlier, the occupation status of these two groups of households dose not differ (Vide Table 5.3). In both the cases about 80 per cent of the households depend on the informal jobs for their livelihood. Hence, not only in the present but also in future these households could not be hoped to improve their economic status, unless some magic happens. Construction activities and Mahatma Gandhi National Rural Employment Programmes (MGNREGP) seem to help the people to earn some income. Otherwise their condition would be still more miserable. Unless government makes some effort to improve the living condition (it cannot be hoped so under the present situation), the people may be forced to take up illegal activities and to live in urban slums of the shining cities in India.

According to the Planning commission, around 80 per cent of tribal population are still working in the primary sectors (2010).

Prasanna and Kurinjmalar's (2017) study exposed that SCs and STs population are more interested to work for MGNREGP to fulfill their basic need like consumption, medical, children education SHGs.

Sakthivel (2017) study found that the major shares of income for the landless households are received through livestock in rural areas..

The study by Soundarpadian and Yamuna (2017) pointed-out that in most of the tribal areas poor transport facility and non-availability of government society, are the reasons for the low price they get for their products.

5.2.4 Types of Houses

There are good cement roads, cement walled houses and tiled roofs. Only a few houses are thatched and with mud walls. On an average the total area in which houses are constructed is 450 sq.ft and the open area for regular use in about 450 sq.ft. Their doors look beautiful with forest woods. They depend on public water connection for water.

There is no significant difference between the two groups of households in terms of the types of houses (Vide Table 5.4). Both groups have almost similar houses. Indra Avaas Yojana (IAY) has helped about 16 per cent of the respondents to have better houses. Still people live in huts and sleep on the roadsides not only in this village but also in many cities in India, which is claimed to have gathered potential for becoming super power in the world.

5.2.5 Drinking Water

For the provision of drinking water, government has made appreciable efforts. Many small over-head tanks-with 1,000 litre capacity each-have been constructed. Besides this a larger-around 10,000 litre capacity-over-head tank is also available for which a well-water is used. The smaller tanks are filled with bore-wells. The NABARD has funded for the construction of over- head tanks.

This village appears to have better water facility. There are 10 wells with over-head tanks and nine hand pumps. All the households have access to drinking water either though private or public connection. In this respect too, the two groups of households do not seems to differ (Vide Table 5.5).

5.2.6 Toilets

The houses constructed by Indhra Awas Yojana (IAY) do have provision for construction of toilets, but the toilets are used for some other purposes. Open defecation is widely present here. More than 90 per cent of the people do not use toilet; they prefer open space. More than 80 per cent of the houses do not have toilets. In this respect too, there is no difference between the two groups of households (Vide Table 5.6). It is to be noted here that the condition as mentioned above is prevalent even with the financial support provide by Central (Rs. 8,000) and State (Rs. 4,000) governments. As on now, totally only 18 households have got toilet facilities and only 8 households use for the purpose it is meant. About 10 households use toilets for other purposes.

As per the WHO and UNICEF (2012) jointly publishing the report says that India accounts for 90 per cent of the (692 million) people in South Asia practice in open defecation. In other hand around 40 per cent of the world population lake of access to safe sanitation and 15 per cent of the population still open defecation.

The study Anupama Nallari (2015) reported that 597 million (or) 48 per cent of the population still practicing open defecation in rural India.

5.2.7 Assets

Assets have been classified into four categories namely, house, land, livestock and durable goods. First the ownership status is given in Table 5.7. Then, the present market values have been used for aggregating the value of the assets (Vide Table 5.8)

All most all the houses own cattle. They keep around 50 per cent of the cattle with them, the value of which have been included in the calculation. The remaining cattle are left in the forest for months together. Only when they are required, they are brought to the houses..

Among the respondents 76 own house in BPL category and 37 own house in the APL category. The mean value of the home for BPLHs and APLHs are Rs. 1.19 lakh and Rs. 1.10 respectively (slightly lower for

APLHs). Z test has been used to test whether the difference is statistically significant. The test shows the differences is not statistically different.

Similar exercise was done for the land, livestock and durable goods. In all of them, the difference was not statistically different. That means, the BPLHs' asset position is almost equal to that of APLHs.

Another important point to be noted is that actually for APLHs the mean value of houses, livestock and durable goods are lower. All the respondents of both categories own houses. Excepting a few almost all the respondents of both categories own land, television, mixer grinder, wet grinder, mobile phone and fans. More than 50 per cent of the both categories own motorbike. In the ownership of the assets and durable goods also the difference between the two groups of households is not statistically significant (vide Table 5.7)

Hence, it could be concluded that the APLHs are not statistically or actually better off than the BPLHs (Vide Table 5.7 and 5.8)

5.2.8 Landholding Size

Landholding size appears to be smaller for BPLHs as compared to that for APLHs. The per capita landholding size for BPLHs and APLHs are 0.62 acre and 0.83 acre respectively. Around 65 per cent of the BPLHs own less than 2.00 acres of land while more than 75 per cent of APLHs own more than 2.00 acres of land. Thus the APLHs are richer in terms of size of landholdings owned (vide Table 5.9).

5.2.9 Income

After major sources of income were identified viz., income from crop cultivation and livestock rearing, secondary occupation like participating in construction activities, the income from these sources have been estimated for the reference year using the current prices. Here, the APLHs have earned significantly larger income as compared to their counterpart viz., BPLHs.

The major crops cultivated are samai, cumbu, cholam, ragi. The samai variety was introduced by Tamil Nadu agricultural university, Coimbatore, in the year 2004. Around 75 percent of harvest products are sold at the spot to private businessmen. In the recent times Sunflower and Tapiocco cultivators are becoming popular.

Of the total income from livestock, a larger amount is earned from sales of animals. Draught power or the livestock products like milk, dung do not find any significant place.

Totally four out of 113 sample households have received two goats, each, worth of Rs. 5,000 per house. However six households have received sums worth of Rs. 30,000 each forwardation and nepotism in selective of beneficiaries cannot be ruled out here.

Of the total household income around 40 per cent comes from agriculture and the remaining 60 per cent comes from varies other jobs. Six girls have received Rs. 60,000 each from government. They are working in spinning mills in Tiruppur. Around 20 persons received old age pensions (Rs. 1,500 per month per person). Only one woman has received marriage financial assistance of Rs. 50,000 and four grams of gold. Since many girls get married before attaining the age of 18 years, they are unable to utilize the scheme of assistance.

As many as 9 women have received maternity benefits and 27 students (20 schools students and seven college students) have received scholarship.In income earning activities, the APLHs are in advantaged situation. They are able to move faster and fare to take up secondary occupations. Since some of the APLHs are located very close to the boundary of the reserve forest, they have easy access to forest products (vide Table 5.10).

The earlier studies have stated that the per capita income for the rural land owned tribal cultivators and landless tribals are Rs. 1,613 and Rs. 1,377 respectively (Karuppaiyan, 1990)

According to the World Bank data around 40 per cent of the BPL households income was US$ 664 (664*50 = 33,200 in Indian Rupee) at the 2011 (PPP) purchasing power parity (2016).

Jayakumar's study also pointed out that the tribal people earn low level of income compared to the Non-ST population, this income not fulfilled their basic needs (2016).

Tribal population received around 20 to 40 per cent of the households income from the forest products. Most of the poor families mostly depend on forest products, but the local market prices are very low in the tribal area (Vedeld 2007).

Chandel, Yadav and Jhariya's (2017) study shows that NTFP (Non-Timber Forest Product) contributed 42 per cent of tribal households income among different sources of forest products like nuts and fruits, medicinal raw materials.

5.2.10 Savings and Borrowings

The respondents do not deposit any money in bank or post office. The money comes through MGNREGS is deposited in the bank. The money not withdrawn from the bank is treated as savings here.

Hospital expenses are the major reason for borrowing. Also some people have used borrowed money for supplementing the construction expenses borne by IAY. Three persons in the sample households have borrowed money for paying fees in college for getting B.Ed degrees.

The surplus money with a temple (Kaliyamman Koil) is also lent to the households at relatively cheaper interest rate.

There is no significant difference between the two groups of households in savings (Vide Table 5.11). However, the size of borrowing differs significantly between the two groups of households. The BPLHs have borrowed significantly larger funds as compared to their counterparts (Vide Table 5.11).

More than 80 per cent of the sample households have opened savings bank (SB) account only to get their wages of MGNREGP thorough bank. Otherwise, the respondents do not seem to show interest in opening account in the banks.

According to census of India 58.7 per cent of total rural India households have accessed banking services (2011).

According to the RBI (Reserve Bank of India) 14 per cent of the Indian Villages use the financial services in both public and private banks (2014).

According to AIDIS SCs, STs and OBCs households are getting less opportunity for finances from the formal institution sources. Most of them depend on the informal financial services like moneylenders, pawnbrokers, etc., in the rural areas (Ahro Kumar Sahoo, 2017).

5.2.11 Expenditure

The high yield varieties of seeds are mostly used. Only for cambu, cholam and ground nuts some quantity of local seeds are used. Next major item of the agricultural cost is fertilizer which is again purchased from the nearest towns. Exchange of labour is predominant. Only about 25 per cent of agricultural labour is purchased by paying money.

Major food items is rice followed by ragi and cumbu. Rice distributed by public distribution system is largely consumed. Earlier rice did not find so much space in the food basket. In the non-food expenditure major portion goes to cloth, cosmetics, health, education and transport.

Total expenditure has been divided into two major categories viz. food and non-food expenditure. Food expenditure has been further divided into six groups and non-food expenditure into five groups. The interesting observation is that in all the eleven groups the per capita expenditure of the APLHs is greater than that for the BPLHs. Some of the groups like expenditure on main food, on non-vegetarians items, on cloths and on crop cultivation are statistically and significantly higher for the APLHs (Vide Table 5.11 and 5.12).

Bhanu (2012) reported that in the developing countries the STs people spend larger amount of income on food consumption.

5.3 Bottom and Top 10 Households

The earlier analysis was based on two groups namely households living BPL and APL. These two groups do not differ significantly in many of the items excepting households size, income, some expenditure items and borrowing. The APLHs have higher landholding and income status; they spend more on consumption and cultivation. Their differences however do not have impact on the lifestyle of the households where both groups of households appear similar. Hence one more method of analysis was attempted. Here, the bottom most and top most 10 households in terms of per capita income were identified for comparison purpose. Now the differences appear to be clear and statistically significant.

5.3.1 Occupation

The top ten households (TTHs) seems to have better occupation status in terms of remuneration whereas the bottom ten households (BTHs) depend on the occupation which yield less remuneration (Vide Table 5.15).

5.3.2 Education

The respondents of TTHs have slightly better educational status. As much as 70 per cent of the respondents of BTHs are still illiterate (Vide Table 5.16).

5.3.3 Housing

There is no significant difference in the type of house between the TTHs and BTHs. In case of toilet use also, the difference is not significant (Vide Table 5.17 and 5.18).

5.3.4 Landholding

Landholding status of TTHs is slightly better than their counterparts; eight households of the bottom group own less than 2 acres of land; this is only six for the BTHs (Vide Table 5.19).

5.3.5 Per capita Income

Five sources of income have been considered. They are income from crop, livestock, forest, government schemes and other sources. The income for TTHs is higher in four categories, excepting category viz, livestock (Vide Table 5.20).

5.3.6 Food Expenditure

Six categories of expenditure were considered under this head. The TTHs spend less on millets and intoxicants as compared to their counterparts. In the remaining four items TTHs spend significantly more as compared to their counterparts viz BTHs (Vide Table 5.21).

5.3.7 Non-food Expenditure

There are five categories under this head. They are expenditure on cloth, education, health, crop cultivation and miscellaneous. The size of expenditure for all the five items are larger for the TTHs (Vide Table 5.22).

5.3.8 Savings and Borrowings

TTHs save more and borrow less. The differences are statistically significant.

5.4. Conclusion

This chapter was set to find out if there is any difference between poor and non-poor households. At the first stage on the basis of per capita income (Rs. 18,125) total sampled households were divided into two groups. Those households earning less than or equal to Rs 18,125 per capita per annum were grouped under Below Poverty Line. And the households with above Rs. 18,125 per capita per annum were considered as living Above Poverty Line. These BPLHs and APLHs are different in terms of income, expenditure, landholding size, savings and borrowing. However they do not seem to differ in their life style, denoted by housing, education, occupation etc..

At the second stage the bottom most and top most 10 households, in terms of per capita income, were put into analysis, to see whether there is any difference between the poor and non-poor households. Now the differences are clear and the TTHs have significantly larger landholdings, income, expenditure savings and smaller borrowing, as compared to BTHs. However, there is no significant difference between the TTHs and BTHs in terms of life styles denoted by housing, education, occupation, etc..

Therefore, it can be concluded that (a) first there is no significant difference between the poor and non-poor households in villages (b) second relatively larger landholdings, income and expenditure of the non-poor households do not have any significant effect on improving their standard of living. The households in villages are almost similar irrespective of their income and landholding size. Hence, to improve the standard of living of the people, larger changes are required.

References:

Ahro Kumar Sahoo (2017): "Determinants of Financial Inclusion in Tribal Disricts of Odisha an Empirical investigation:, Social Changes, Sage Publication, 47 (1), Pp. 45-64.

Amulya Kumar Benerat (2015): "Primary Education Among Tribal People of Mayurbhanj District of Odisha: An Evaluative Study," International Journal of Humanities and Social Science Invention, Vol. 4, Issue 2, Pp. 43-54.

Anupama Nallari (2015): "All We Want are Toilets Inside our Home," Environment & Urbanization, Vol. 27, No.1, Pp. 73-88.

Asha Sasidharan (2017): "Livelihood Transition: Socio-Cultural and Economic Impacts on Tribal Life," Journal of Social Work Education and Practice, Vol. 2 (3), Iss: 2456-2068, Pp. 09-17.

Census of India (2011): "Government of India."

Chandel, Yadav, and Jhariya (2017): "Economically and Traditionally Important Non-Timber Forest Products of Sarguja Division," Bulletin of Environment, Pharmacology and life sciences, Vol.6 (5), Pp. 32-39.

Karuppaiyan. E, (2,1990):, "Alienation of tribal land in Tamil Nadu," Economic and Political Weekly, Vol-25, No-22, pp-1185-1186

Prasanna and Kurinjmalar (2017): "Impact of MGNREGP on poverty Alleviation in rural India A Case Study of Two districts in Tamil Nadu," Journal of Academia and Industrial Research (JAIR), Vol.5, Issue 9, Pp. 139-142.

Sathivel (2017): "Role and Contribution of Livestock in Livelihood of Marginal and Landless Livestock Farmers in Rural Tamil Nadu, India," Indian Res. J. Ext. Edu., (Special issue on Veterinary Research & Extension), Pp. 20-25.

Soundarpadian and Yamuna (2017): "Role of Non-Timber Forest Products in Poverty Reduction Among Tribals in Western Ghats of Tamil Nadu," Asian Journal for Poverty Studies, Vol. 3 (2), Pp. 53-58.

Vedeld, Angelsen, Bojo (2007): "Forest Environmental Income and the Rural Poor," Forest Policy and Economics, Vol. 9 (7), Pp. 869-879.

Rajasekhar, Manjula, Suchitra (2017): "Microfinance promote livelihoods and Reduce Vulnerability, Among Adivasis: A study of some NGOs Interventions from Karnataka and Tamil Nadu," Social change, Vol. 47 (1), Sage Publications, Pp. 65-80.

World Bank (2016): "Poverty and Shared Prosperity Taking on Inequality," Libratory of Congress Cataloging In-publication data has been applied, ISBN- 978-1-4648-0958-3.

Chapter VI

Conclusion

6.1 Introduction

The aim of the study was to see whether there is any difference between poor and non-poor households. More specifically the research question was to see whether the non-poor households have better lifestyle and standard of living than the poor households. For this purpose an empirical context was chosen in the Jawadhu Hills, because the poverty is severe among the tribal population. The revenue village chosen was Puliyur.

The study village consists of a few hamlets. Totally 113 households were drawn from all the households. These households were classified as households living BPL and APL. The number of BPLHs was 76 and APLHs was 37. Poverty line was defined as income of Rs. 50 per day per person.

For these households some of the major aspects were looked into. The APLHs were slightly better than the BPLHs in terms of landholdings, earnings, savings and borrowings. However, there is no statistically significant difference between these two groups of households in terms of lifestyle or standard of livings.

Second attempt was made to see whther there is any significant difference among the bottom most and top most households. On the basis of per capita income, the top most ten households and bottom most ten households were identified, and, compared. Again the TTHs were slightly better than the BTHs in terms of landholdings, earnings, savings, and borrowings. However it cannot be said that the TTHs have better standard of living.

6.2 Policy implications

Form this study; it is clear that standard of living and lifestyle of the tribals may not improve even if their earnings increase. Hence, unless the government does some intervention, the tribal people will continue to lead the same kind of life or take the terrorists path.

6.3 Scope for further research

The findings relate to a particular reference year and particular tribal village namely Puliyur. There may be slight or larger differences in other villages with varying levels of infrastructure, contacts and economic status. In order to validate the conclusion of the present study, more such study need to be taken up in different places and in different points of time.

Tables

Table 5.1 Household Details

Si. No	Item	BPL	APL
1	Income limit (Per day, Per person)	≤Rs.18,250	Rs. 18,251≥
2	Number of Households	76	37
3	Number of persons	349	130
4	Number of Saanar Households	30	4
5	Number of Vellalar Households	46	33
6	Number of joint families	35	15
7	Number of nuclear families	41	22

Source: Compiled data from field survey.

Table 5.2 Respondents' Education

Si. No	Level of Education of Head of the Households / Respondent	Nature of respondents	
		BPL	APL
1	Illiterate	50	20
2	Primary	10 (13.15)	3 (8.10)
3	Upper Primary	10 (13.15)	8 (21.62)
4	Secondary	5 (6.57)	2 (5.41)
5	Higher secondary	Nil	Nil
6	UG	Nil	1
7	PG and above	1 (1.31)	3 (8.10)
	Total	76	37

Source: Compiled data from field survey.

Table 5.3 Respondents' Occupations

Si. No	Major Occupations of respondents	Nature of respondents			
		BPL		APL	
		Main	Secondary	Main	Secondary
1	No occupation	1(1.4)	2 (2.6)	Nil	2 (5.4)
2	Cultivators	75 (98.6)	1 (1.3)	35(94.6)	Nil
3	Agricultural labour	Nil	3 (3.9)	Nil	1 (2.7)
4	Government job	Nil	1 (1.3)	Nil	1 (2.7)
5	Construction work	Nil	35 (46.0)	2 (5.4)	19 (51.35)
6	MGNREGA	Nil	34 (44.7)	Nil	14 (37.83)
	Total	76 (100)	76 (100)	37 (100)	37 (100)

Source: Compiled data from field survey.

Table 5.4 Types of Houses (Ref. year)

Si. No	Type of houses	Nature of respondents	
		BPL	APL
1	Hut	0	3 (8.10)
2	Kucha	10 (13.15)	2 (5.40)
3	Semi pucca	33 (43.42)	16 (43.24)
4	Pucca	17 (22.36)	6 (16.21)
5	IAY house	16 (21.05)	10 (27.02)
	Total	76 (100)	37 (100)

Source: Compiled data from field survey.

Note: (IAY) Indira Awaas Yojana

Table 5.5 Drinking Water Connection

Si. No	Type of Families	Own Water Connection	Public Water Connection
		Yes	No
1	BPL families (No.)	57	19
2	APL families(No.)	29	8
	Total (No.)	86	27

Source: Compiled data from field survey.

Table 5.6 Toilets and usage of toilets

Si. No	Item	No. of HHS			
		BPL		APL	
		Yes	No	Yes	No
1	Toilet	14 (18.42)	62(81.57)	4 (10.81)	33 (89.18)
2	Usage of toilet	6 (7.89)	8 (10.52)	2 (5.40)	2 (5.40)
3	Open defecation	70 (92.10)		35 (94.59)	

Source: Compiled data from field survey.

Table 5.7 Household Assets Holdings (Ref. year)

Si. No	Item	No. of HHS			
		BPL		APL	
		Yes	No	Yes	No
1	House	76	-	37	-
2	Landholding	73	3	36	1
3	Television	76	0	37	0
4	Mixer grinder	74	2	36	1
5	Wet grinder	73	3	36	1
6	Laptop	9	67	7	30
7	Mobile phone	73	3	33	4
8	Motorbike	42	35	20	17
9	Bicycle	25	51	11	26
10	Emergency lamp	37	40	23	14
11	Fan	75	1	36	1

Source: Compiled data from field survey.

Table 5.8 Households Assets in Money term (Rs., Ref. year)

Si. No	Assets	BPL		APL		Zc- test value	Sig. / NS.
		Mean	SD	Mean	SD		
1	House	1,19,342	75,953	1,10,742	87,942	0.58	NS.
2	Land	2,29,605	1,34,208	2,68,919	1,83,844	1.15	NS.
3	Livestock	26,161	28,062	25,695	23,287	0.09	NS.
4	Durable goods	30,290	23,702	27,850	18,159	0.60	NS.

Source: Compiled data from field survey.

Note: *Sig- significant. **NS- Not Significant.

Table 5.9 Household landholding size.

Si. No	Size of land	No. of HHS	
		BPL	APL
1	No land	3 (3.9)	1 (2.70)
2	Less than 1 acre	14 (18.42)	7 (18.91)
3	1.1 to 2 acre	32 (42.10)	7 (18.91)
4	2.1 to 3 acre	15 (19.73)	13 (35.13)
5	3.1 to 4 acre	4 (5.26)	7 (18.91)
6	4.1 to 5 acre	7 (9.21)	6 (16.21)
7	5.1 and above	5 (6.57)	3 (8.10)

Source: Compiled data from field survey.

Table 5.10 Per Capita Income from Different Sources (Rs. Ref. year)

Si. No	Income sources	BPL		APL		Zc- test value	Sig. / NS.
		Mean	SD	Mean	SD		
1	Crop income per acre	4,193	2,531.35	10,968	8.746.70	4.56	Sig.
2	Livestock	245	800.86	178	671.16	0.44	NS.
3	Secondary occupation	5,739	3,289.92	14,741	7,966.06	7.37	Sig.
4	Forest	882	1,390.47	1,006	1,417.65	0.56	NS.
5	Govt. scheme	784	1,123.73	1,946	3,181.58	0.79	NS.

Source: Compiled data from field survey.

Note: *Sig- significant. **NS- Not Significant.

Table 5.11 Per Capita Food Expenditure (Rs. Ref. year)

Si. No	Item	BPL		APL		Zc- test value	Sig. / NS.
		Mean	SD	Mean	SD		
1	Expenditure on main food (Rs.)	2,082	1,054.49	2,860	1,016.01	4.10	Sig.
2	Expenditure On Millets (Rs.)	272	301.56	343	405.56	0.01	NS.
3	Expenditure On Spices and pulses (Rs.)	1,299	527.66	1,746	639.01	3.91	Sig.

Si. No	Item	BPL		APL		Zc-test value	Sig. / NS.	Si. No	Item
		Mean	SD	Mean	SD				
4	Expenditure On Non-veg (Rs.)	947		449.41		1,365	610	2.61	Sig.
5	Expenditure on intoxicants (Rs.)	287		538.96		1,218	4,913	0.10	NS.
6	Expenditure on ready to eat food (Rs.)	432		219.39		606	285.30	2.54	Sig.

Source: compiled data from field survey.

Note: *Sig- significant. **NS- Not Significant.

Table 5.12 Per Capita Non-food Expenditure (Rs. Ref. year)

Si. No	Item	BPL		APL		Zc-test value	Sig. / NS.
		Mean	SD	Mean	SD		
1	Exp. on cloths& cosmetics (Rs.)	1,749	597.35	2,129	950.12	2.26	Sig.
2	Exp. on miscellanies (Rs.)	2,284	1,908.49	2,700	1,141.47	0.91	NS.
3	Exp. on education (Rs.)	1,181	2,658.23	1,052	2,117.13	0.20	NS.
4	Exp. on Health (Rs.)	2,511	2,117.14	3,281	2,562.88	1.73	NS.
5	Expenditure on crop (Rs. Ref. year) (Rs.)	308	653.66	2,010	1,321.97	5.60	Sig.

Source: Compiled data from field survey.

Note: *Sig- significant. **NS- Not Significant.

Table 5.13 Per capita savings and borrowing (Ref. year, Rs.)

Si. No	Item	No. of households in BPL		No. of households in APL		BPL		APL		Zc-test value	Sig. / NS.
		Yes	No	Yes	No	Mean	SD	Mean	SD		
1	Savings (Rs.)	61	15	37	-	308	653.66	636	1,321.97	1.42	NS.
2	Borrowed money (Rs.)	40	36	14	23	5,848	10,773.48	3,173	4,854.93	3.01	Sig

Source: Compiled data from field survey.

Note: *Sig- significant. **NS- Not Significant.

Table 5.14 Number of Households Benefited from Government Schemes (Ref. year)

Si. No	Name of the schemes	BPL	APL
1	Old Age Pension	14 (18.42)	6 (16.21)
2	Marriage found	1 (1.31)	Nil
3	Maternal benefit scheme	6 (7.89)	3 (8.10)
4	Scholarship	18 (23.68)	9 (24.32)
5	Livestock assistances to govt.	3 (3.94)	2 (5.40)

Source: Compiled data from field survey.

Table 5.15 Main and secondary occupation of bottom 10 HHs and top 10HHs

Si. No	Occupation	Bottom		Top	
		Main	Secondary	Main	Secondary
1	No occupation	-	1	-	2
2	Cultivation	10	1	8	-
3	Agricultural labour	-	1	-	-
4	Construction labour	-	1	2	5
5	MGNREGA	-	6	-	3

Source: Compiled data from field survey.

Table 5.16 Respondent education of bottom 10 HHs and top 10HHs

Si. No	Education	No. of respondents	
		Bottom	Top
1	Illiterate	7	3
2	Primary	-	1
3	Upper primary	2	2
4	Highs school	1	2
5	UG / PG with Bed.,	-	2

Source: Compiled data from field survey.

Table 5.17 Type of house of bottom 10 HHs and top 10HHs

Si. No	Type of house	No. of respondents	
		Bottom	Top
1	Hut	-	1
2	Kutch	3	2
3	Semi-Pucca	2	2
4	Pucca	3	2
5	IAY	2	3

Source: Compiled data from field survey.

Table 5.18 Toilets availability and usage of toilets of bottom 10 HHs and top 10HHs

Si. No	Items	Bottom10 HHs		Top10 HHs	
		Yes	No	Yes	No
1	Toilets	4	6	1	9
2	Usage of toilets	1	9	0	10

Source: Compiled data from field survey.

Table 5.19 Landholding of top 10 HHs and bottom 10 HHs

Si. No	Size of land	Bottom10 HHs	Top10 HHs
1	No land	-	1
2	0-1	3	3
3	1.1 to 2	5	2
4	2.1 to 3	2	3
5	3.1 and above	-	1

Source: Compiled data from field survey.

Table 5.20 Per Capita income of top 10 HHs and bottom 10 HHs (Ref. year, Rs.)

Si. No	Income sources	Bottom 10 HHs		Top 10 HHs		Zc- test value	Sig. / NS.
		Mean	SD	Mean	SD		
1	Crop income per acre	1,947	1,265.92	16,188	14,484.75	1.70	NS.
2	Livestock	300	948.68	85	271.05	0.89	NS.
3	Secondary occupation	1,928	1,052.69	22,602	8,950.23	6.64	Sig
4	Forest	402	444.87	1,323	2,119.50	0.85	NS.
5	Govt. scheme	101	245.52	3,583	4,864.36	1.96	NS.

Source: Compiled data from field survey.

Note: *Sig- significant. **NS- Not Significant.

Table 5.21 Per Capita food expenditure of top 10 HHs and bottom 10 HHs (Ref. year, Rs.)

Si. No	Item	Bottom 10 HHs		Top 10 HHs		Zc- test value	Sig. / NS.
		Mean	SD	Mean	SD		
1	Expenditure on main food (Rs.)	1,714	439.49	3,172	1,298	3.95	Sig.
2	Expenditure On Millets (Rs.)	212	151.44	163	285.64	2.85	Sig.
3	Expenditure On spices (Rs.)	1051	399.81	1,874	527.03	2.39	Sig.
4	Expenditure On meat (Rs.)	725	257.90	1,405	644.34	2.22	Sig.
5	Expenditure on intoxicants (Rs.)	240	623.97	123	261.98	1.05	NS.
6	Expenditure on ready to eat food (Rs.)	338	131.67	695	352.13	2.37	Sig.

Source: Compiled data from field survey.

Note: *Sig- significant. **NS- Not Significant.

Table 5.22 Per Capita Non-food Expenditure of top 10 HHs and bottom 10 HHs (Ref. year, Rs.)

Si. No	Item	Bottom 10 HHs		Top 10 HHs		Zc- test value	Sig. / NS.
		Mean	SD	Mean	SD		
1	Exp. on cloths& cosmetics (Rs.)	1,296	368.28	2,636	1,386.33	2.78	Sig.
2	Exp. on miscellanies (Rs.)	3,268	5,047.55	3,431	1494.84	1.59	NS.
3	Exp. on education (Rs.)	140	154.27	459	984.84	0.69	NS.
4	Exp. on Health (Rs.)	2,917	3,351.67	3,209	1,605.44	1.81	NS.
5	Expenditure on crop (Rs. Ref. year) (Rs.)	426	298.11	2,726	2,059.99	1.18	NS.

Source: Compiled data from field survey.

Note: *Sig- significant. **NS- Not Significant.

Table 5. 23 Per capita savings and borrowing of top 10 HHs and bottom 10 HHs (Ref. year, Rs.)

Si. No	Item	Bottom 10 HHs		Top 10 HHs		Zc- test value	Sig. / NS.
		Mean	SD	Mean	SD		
1	Savings (Rs.)	186	398.28	1,031	1,753.96	568.77	Sig.
2	Borrowed money (Rs.)	5,923	8,696.22	1,666	5,270.46	3215.61	Sig.

Source: Compiled data from field survey.
Note: *Sig- significant. **NS- Not Significant.

Table 5. 24 Total income and expenditure of the APL households (in 000)

S. No	Total Receipts (TR)			Total Expenditures (TE)					Differences in (TR-TE)	Per capita Differences
	Total Inco-me	Borro-wed money	Total receip-ts	Total food expendit-ure	Total Non-food expendit-ure	Crop expendit-ure	Savin-gs	Total expendit-ure	HHs Differen-ces amount	
1	117.0	0	117.0	11.6	30.0	10.0	7.0	58.6	58.4	11.6
2	102.5	0	102.5	18.6	23.0	5.0	0	46.6	55.8	11.1
3	150.0	0	150.0	27.8	23.2	15.0	0	66.0	83.9	20.9
4	46.0	0	46.0	7.1	8.5	5.0	0.1	20.7	25.3	12.6
5	307.0	0	307.0	25.0	52.5	10.0	5.0	92.5	214.5	107.2
6	130.5	0	130.5	22.8	46.6	15.0	0	84.4	46.1	9.2
7	83.5	0	83.5	13.9	20.5	0	0	34.4	49.1	12.2
8	80.0	0	80.0	22.0	17.0	2.0	10.0	51.0	29.0	4.8
9	95.0	50.0	145.0	25.4	17.5	2.0	2.0	46.9	98.1	32.7
10	94.0	0	94.0	15.9	21.0	5.0	1.0	42.9	51.1	10.2
11	89.5	0	89.5	20.7	16.5	10.0	0	47.2	42.3	7.0
12	87.0	50.0	137.0	23.4	43.0	6.0	0	72.4	64.6	32.3
13	87.0	0	87.0	22.8	29.0	7.0	0	58.8	28.2	5.6
14	83.6	0	83.6	28.9	28.0	7.0	0	63.9	19.7	6.5
15	107.0	0	107.0	22.6	32.0	6.0	0	60.6	46.4	7.7
16	104.2	10.0	114.2	26.4	36.7	5.0	13.5	81.6	32.5	8.1
17	51.2	0	51.2	11.6	10.0	4.0	0	25.6	25.6	8.5
18	73.5	20.0	93.5	32.8	51.5	6.0	1.0	91.3	2.2	0.7
19	97.5	0	97.5	24.1	76.6	2.5	5.0	108.2	-10.7	-2.6
20	73.0	20.0	93.0	26.2	19.0	1.5	0	46.7	46.3	15.4

S. No	Total Receipts (TR			Total Expenditures (TE)					Differences in (TR-TE)	Per capita Differences
	Total Income	Borrowed money	Total receipts	Total food expenditure	Total Non-food expenditure	Crop expenditure	Savings	Total expenditure	HHs Differences amount	
21	70.0	30.0	100.0	15.0	13.0	10.0	2.0	40.0	60.0	30.0
22	92.3	25.0	117.3	32.0	54.0	8.5	0	94.5	22.8	5.7
23	137.0	0	137.0	25.1	13.0	10.0	0	48.1	88.9	22.2
24	67.9	0	67.9	32.0	11.5	3.0	0	46.5	21.4	7.1
25	113.0	40.0	153.0	32.0	25.5	8.0	2.0	67.5	85.5	28.5
26	135.0	0	135.0	22.0	50.0	16.0	1.5	89.5	45.5	15.1
27	45.0	0	45.0	14.2	14.0	4.5	1.0	33.7	11.3	3.7
28	111.5	0	111.5	26.0	29.0	5.0	0	60.0	51.5	17.1
29	65.1	20.0	85.1	37.5	23.0	3.0	0	63.5	21.6	7.2
30	126.0	50.0	176.0	31.6	81.0	8.0	2.0	122.6	53.4	26.7
31	81.0	30.0	111.0	27.6	52.2	3.0	0	82.8	28.2	14.1
32	101.0	25.0	126.0	31.0	34.1	5.0	2.0	72.1	53.9	17.9
33	40.0	0	40.0	17.5	15.0	6.0	0	38.5	1.5	0.2
34	40.0	25.0	65.0	86.2	27.5	3.0	1.0	117.7	-52.7	-52.7
35	79.3	0	79.3	30.5	44.0	8.0	20.0	102.5	-23.2	-7.7
36	93.5	20.0	113.5	25.4	49.0	10.0	0	84.4	29.1	14.5
37	92.0	0	92.0	27.0	26.0	5.0	1.0	59.0	33.0	16.5

Source: Compiled data from field survey.

Table 5. 25 Total income and expenditure of the BPL households (in 000)

S. No	Total Receipts (TR)			Total Expenditures (TE)					Differences in (TR-TE)	Per capita differences
	Total income	Borrowed money	Total receipts	Crop Expenditure	Food expenditure	Non-food expenditure	savings	Total expenditure	Differences amount	
1	16.3	25.0	41.3	2.0	18.0	30.3	0	50.3	-9.0	-1.2
2	12.0	100.0	112.0	0	15.0	39.4	5.0	59.4	52.6	13.1
3	15.0	0	15.0	0	16.7	80.0	0	96.7	-81.7	-20.4
4	28.5	100.0	128.5	3.0	22.5	13.5	0	39.0	89.5	14.9
5	29.8	0	29.8	3.5	15.2	18.0	0	36.7	-6.9	-1.1
6	30.0	0	30.0	2.0	28.8	28.5	2.5	61.8	-31.8	-6.3
7	26.8	50.0	76.8	2.0	26.4	38.0	0	66.4	10.4	2.0
8	28.7	0	28.7	3.0	24.2	34.5	0	61.7	-33.0	-6.6
9	29.5	20.0	49.5	2.8	36.0	74.7	1.0	114.5	-65.0	-13.0
10	30.0	0	30.0	5.0	19.6	13.0	0	37.6	-7.6	-1.9
11	24.7	30.0	54.7	2.0	23.0	17.3	0	42.3	12.4	2.0
12	40.0	25.0	65.0	5.0	28.8	23.0	0	56.8	8.2	1.3
13	37.3	200.0	237.3	2.5	29.2	42.0	0	73.7	163.6	32.7
14	53.7	0	53.7	5.0	38.4	21.5	0	64.9	-11.2	-1.6
15	46.6	70.0	116.6	3.0	20.9	33.5	0	57.4	59.2	9.8
16	23.5	200.0	223.5	1.0	15.0	23.0	0	39.0	184.5	61.5
17	16.5	0	16.5	0	10.6	15.1	1.0	26.7	-10.2	-5.1
18	33.5	0	33.5	3.0	33.4	33.0	0	69.4	-35.9	-8.9
19	51.0	0	51.0	2.0	26.4	80.0	5.0	113.4	-62.4	-10.4

S. No	Total Receipts (TR			Total Expenditures (TE)					Differences in (TR-TE)	Per capita differences
	Total income	Borrowed money	Total receipts	Crop Expenditure	Food expenditure	Non-food expenditure	savings	Total expenditure	Differences amount	
20	35.0	30.0	65.0	2.0	20.4	36.5	1.0	59.9	5.1	1.2
21	53.0	10.0	63.0	3.0	26.8	31.7	0.5	62.0	1.0	0.1
22	26.5	0	26.5	2.5	10.6	12.5	0	25.6	0.9	0.3
23	44.7	30.0	74.7	2.0	26.2	28.0	0	56.2	18.5	3.7
24	9.0	0	9.0	0	4.5	5.0	0	9.5	-0.5	-0.5
25	45.0	50.0	95.0	8.0	39.6	41.0	2.0	90.6	4.4	0.8
26	38.2	30.0	68.2	5.0	23.0	32.0	0	60.0	8.2	2.0
27	61.0	50.0	111.0	2.0	21.9	31.8	2.0	57.7	53.2	8.8
28	52.5	100.0	152.5	6.0	26.0	49.0	0	81.0	71.5	14.3
29	63.5	25.0	88.5	3.0	21.2	51.6	8.0	83.8	4.7	0.7
30	64.0	0	64.0	3.0	25.4	20.0	0	48.4	15.6	2.6
31	43.0	0	43.0	3.0	19.0	33.0	0	55.0	-12.0	-3.0
32	43.2	0	43.2	5.0	16.8	27.0	1.0	49.8	-6.6	-1.6
33	32.5	0	32.5	3.0	19.2	21.0	0	43.2	-10.7	-3.5
34	68.5	0	68.5	3.0	26.7	57.8	1.0	88.5	-20.0	-3.3
35	59.5	30.0	89.5	4.5	22.4	25.5	5.0	57.4	32.1	6.4
36	36.0	0	36.0	4.5	12.7	12.0	0	29.2	6.8	2.2
37	85.8	0	85.8	4.0	25.5	33.5	15.0	78.0	7.8	1.1
38	75.0	0	75.0	5.0	16.9	26.5	0	48.4	26.6	4.4
39	76.0	0	76.0	4.0	20.8	18.5	1.0	44.3	31.7	5.2
40	38.2	100.0	138.2	4.0	25.3	15.0	0	44.3	93.9	31.3
41	65.5	0	65.5	3.0	17.2	22.0	2.5	44.7	20.8	4.1

S. No	Total Receipts (TR			Total Expenditures (TE)					Differences in (TR-TE)	Per capita differences
	Total income	Borrowed money	Total receipts	Crop Expenditure	Food expenditure	Non-food expenditure	savings	Total expenditure	Differences amount	
42	65.5	0	65.5	2.5	25.4	41.0	1.0	69.9	-4.4	-0.8
43	52.5	80.0	132.5	2.0	24.0	26.5	0	52.5	80.0	20.0
44	79.9	0	79.9	2.0	35.4	60.7	0	98.1	-18.2	-3.0
45	40.0	50.0	90.0	4.0	21.2	10.0	0	35.2	54.8	18.2
46	67.0	10.0	77.0	5.0	20.2	28.0	1.0	54.2	22.8	4.5
47	68.6	0	68.6	5.0	27.8	119.0	10.0	161.8	-93.2	-18.6
48	69.0	10.0	79.0	2.0	28.2	34.0	0	64.2	14.8	2.9
49	70.0	30.0	100.0	5.5	12.6	60.0	2.0	80.1	19.9	3.9
50	84.0	0	84.0	5.0	26.8	67.0	5.0	103.8	-19.8	-3.3
51	71.2	20.0	91.2	6.0	23.5	30.0	0	59.5	31.7	6.3
52	71.6	50.0	121.6	2.0	23.0	36.0	2.0	63.0	58.6	29.3
53	43.0	0	43.0	2.5	48.4	54.0	0	104.9	-61.9	-12.3
54	29.0	0	29.0	2.5	8.0	12.0	0	22.5	6.5	3.2
55	88.0	70.0	158.0	3.0	27.2	51.5	0.5	82.2	75.8	12.6
56	44.0	25.0	69.0	2.5	24.2	26.5	0	53.2	15.8	5.2
57	74.9	0	74.9	28.0	18.8	45.0	7.5	74.1	0.8	0.1
58	62.0	0	62.0	4.5	18.2	15.0	0	37.7	24.3	6.0
59	62.5	10.0	72.5	2.0	26.0	24.9	1.0	53.9	18.6	4.6
60	94.0	0	94.0	3.0	36.5	31.3	25.0	95.8	-1.8	-0.3
61	94.0	50.0	144.0	4.0	24.2	51.5	10.0	89.7	54.3	9.0
62	47.2	0	47.2	3.0	27.8	18.4	0	49.2	-2.0	-0.6
63	63.0	0	63.0	5.0	21.6	29.0	0.5	56.1	6.9	1.7

S. No	Total Receipts (TR			Total Expenditures (TE)					Differences in (TR-TE)	Per capita differences
	Total income	**Borrowed money**	**Total receipts**	**Crop Expenditure**	**Food expenditure**	**Non-food expenditure**	**savings**	**Total expenditure**	**Differences amount**	
64	96.0	0	96.0	6.0	14.4	24.0	0	44.4	51.6	8.6
65	80.0	75.0	155.0	0	36.2	28.8	1.0	66.0	89.0	17.8
66	80.2	0	80.2	3.0	19.7	20.2	0	42.9	37.3	7.4
67	64.8	0	64.8	2.5	27.6	78.6	1.0	109.7	-44.9	-11.2
68	49.4	50.0	99.4	4.0	24.4	50.5	1.0	79.9	19.5	6.5
69	33.0	5.0	38.0	3.0	12.8	15.5	0	31.3	6.7	3.3
70	49.8	0	49.8	5.0	35.7	55.0	0.5	96.2	-46.3	-15.4
71	66.5	0	66.5	3.0	20.8	19.5	1.0	44.3	22.2	5.5
72	86.5	20.0	106.5	2.0	18.6	41.5	0	62.1	44.4	8.8
73	71.0	0	71.0	3.0	15.2	22.5	0	40.7	30.3	7.5
74	71.0	75.0	146.0	4.5	29.2	68.0	1.0	102.7	43.3	10.8
75	71.7	0	71.7	4.0	24.6	21.5	0	50.1	21.6	5.4
76	36.0	0	36.0	1.8	12.0	11.0	0	24.8	11.2	5.6

Source: Compiled data from field survey.

Table5.26 Income and Expenditure of the Top ten households (in 000)

S. No	Total Receipts (TR)			Total Expenditures (TE)					Differences in (TR-TE)	Per capita
	Total income	Borrowed money	Total receipts	Crop Expenditure	Food expenditure	Non-food expenditure	savings	Total expenditure	Differences amount	Differences
1	117.0	0	117.0	10.0	11.6	30.0	7.0	58.6	58.4	19.4
2	102.5	0	102.5	5.0	18.6	23.0	0	46.6	55.9	18.6
3	150.0	0	150.0	15.0	27.8	23.3	0	66.0	83.9	41.9
4	46.0	0	46.0	5.0	7.1	8.5	0.1	20.7	25.3	12.6
5	307.0	0	307.0	10.0	25.0	52.5	5.0	92.5	214.5	71.5
6	130.5	0	130.5	15.0	22.8	46.6	0	84.4	46.1	6.5
7	83.5	0	83.5	0	13.9	20.5	0	34.4	49.1	49.1
8	80.0	0	80.0	2.0	22.0	17.0	10.0	51.0	29.0	9.6
9	95.0	50.0	145.0	2.0	25.4	17.5	2.0	46.9	98.1	49.0
10	94.0	0	94.0	5.0	15.9	21.0	1.0	42.9	51.1	25.5

Source: Compiled data from field survey.

Table 5.27 Income and Expenditure of the Bottom ten households (in 000)

Si. No	Total Receipts (TR)			Total Expenditures (TE)					Differences in (TR-TE)	Per capita Differences
	Total income	Borrowed money	Total Receipt	Crop exp.	Food exp.	Non-food exp.	savings	Total exp.	HHs Differences	
1	16.3	25.0	41.3	2.0	18.0	30.3	0	50.3	-9.0	-1.2
2	12.0	100.0	112.0	0	15.0	39.4	5.0	59.4	52.6	13.1
3	28.5	100.0	128.5	3.0	22.5	13.5	0	39.0	89.5	22.3
4	15.0	0	15.0	0	16.7	80.0	0	96.7	-81.7	-13.6
5	29.8	0	29.8	3.5	15.2	18.0	0	36.7	-6.9	-1.1
6	30.0	0	30.0	2.0	28.8	28.6	2.5	61.9	-31.9	-5.3
7	26.8	50.0	76.8	2.0	26.4	38.0	0	66.4	10.4	2.0
8	28.7	0	28.7	3.0	24.2	34.5	0	61.7	-33.0	-6.6
9	29.5	20.0	49.5	2.8	36.0	74.7	1.0	114.5	-65.0	-13.0
10	30.0	0	30.0	5.0	19.6	13.0	0	37.6	-7.6	-1.5

Source: Compiled data from field survey.

Table 5. 28 Differences between per capita income and expenditure of APL & BPL households.

Si. No	Item	APL HHs		BPL HHs		Zc- test value	Sig. / NS.
		Mean	SD	Mean	SD		
1	Differences in income and expenditure	18,214	21,334	3,797	11,744	37.023	Sig

Source: Compiled data from field survey.

Note: *Sig- significant. **NS- Not Significant.

Table 5.29 Differences between per capita income and expenditure of Top ten & Bottom ten households.

Si. No	Item	Top ten HHs		Bottom ten HHs		Zc- test value	Sig. / NS.
		Mean	SD	Mean	SD		
1	Differences in income and expenditure	30,417	21,382	-488	11,091	122.86	Sig

Source: Compiled data from field survey.

Note: *Sig- significant. **NS- Not Significant.

Bibliography

Ahluwalia, M. S. (1978): "Rural Poverty and Agricultural Performance in India," Journal of Development Studies, 14(3), pp. 298-303.

Ahluwalia, M. S. (1986): "Rural Poverty Agricultural Production and Prices: A Re-examination in Agricultural Change and Rural Poverty Variations on a Theme by Dharm Narain, John W. Mellor & Gunwant Desal (eds.), Oxford University Press, Bombay.

Ahro Kumar Sahoo (2017): "Determinants of Financial Inclusion in Tribal Disricts of Odisha an Empirical investigation:, Social Changes, Sage Publication, 47 (1), Pp. 45-64.

Alkire, S., and Seth, S. (2008): "Multidimensional Poverty Measurement and BPL Methods in India: A Comparison of Methods," Oxford University: Oxford Poverty and Human Development Initiative, (Working Paper No15).

Amulya Kumar Benerat (2015): "Primary Education Among Tribal People of Mayurbhanj District of Odisha: An Evaluative Study," International Journal of Humanities and Social Science Invention, Vol. 4, Issue 2, Pp. 43-54.

Anderson, J. B. (2003): "The U.S.-Mexico Border: A Half Century of Change," Social Science Journal, Vol. 40 (4), pp. 535-554.

Anju Bala (2018): "Tribes in India: The regional analysis," International Journal of Advanced Research and Development, Volume 3, Issue 1, pp. 54-57.

Anupama Nallari (2015): "All We Want are Toilets Inside our Home," Environment & Urbanization, Vol. 27, No.1, Pp. 73-88.

Asha Sasidharan (2017): "Livelihood Transition: Socio-Cultural and Economic Impacts on Tribal Life," Journal of Social Work Education and Practice, Vol. 2 (3), Iss: 2456-2068, Pp. 09-17.

Aravind K. R. (2008): "An Economic Analysis of Poverty and Livelihood Security among Rural Households in Dharmapuri District of Tamil Nadu," Unpublished M.Sc.(Ag.) Thesis submitted to Department of Agricultural Economics, Tamil Nadu Agricultural University, Coimbatore.

Atul Goswami (1984): "Tribal Development with Special Reference to North-East India," Social Scientist, Vol. 12, No. 8, pp. 55-60.

Balamurugan, P. & Iyyampillai, S. (2005): "Fruit and Vegetable Processing Industry: Some Issues," Southern Economist, 44(12), pp. 21-23.

Batcheldar (1971): "The Economics of Poverty," John Willey and Sons Publications, New York.

Batcheldar (1971): “The Economics of Poverty,” John Willey and Sons Publications, New York.

Basanta K. Pradhan, P. K Ray, M. R. Saluja and Shanta Venkaram (2000): “Rural-Urban Disparities: Income Distribution, Expenditure Pattern and Social Sector,” Economic and Political Weekly, Vol. 35, No. 28/29, pp. 2527-2529+2531-2539.

Bishnoi (1966): “Pattern of Employment and Nature and Causes of Unemployment in Agriculture,” Indian Journal of Agricultural Economics, 21(1), pp. 51-61.

Bourguignon, F. and Chakravarty (2003): “The Measurement of Multidimensional Poverty,” Journal of Economic Inequality, Vol. 1, pp. 25–49.

Census (2011): Office of the Registrar General, Government of India.

Chandel, Yadav, and Jhariya (2017): “Economically and Traditionally Important Non-Timber Forest Products of Sarguja Division,” Bulletin of Environment, Pharmacology and life sciences, Vol.6 (5), Pp. 32-39.

Chandrasekhar, Mousumi Das and Ajay Sharma (2014): “Short-term Migration and Consumption Expenditure of Households in Rural India,” Indira Gandhi Institute of Development Research, Mumbai. http://www.igidr .ac.in/pdf/publication/WP-2014-009.pdf. accessed data, 25-10-2016.

Dandekar, V. M., & Rath, R. (1971): “Poverty in India, Dimensions and Trends.” Economic and Political Weekly, Vol.6, No. 1, pp. 25-48.

Deaton and Dreze (2002): “Poverty and Inequality in India: A Re-Examination,” Economic and Political Weekly, Vol. 37, pp. 3729-3748.

Datt, G., and Ravillion, M. (1989): “Region Disparities, Targetion and Poverty in India,” World Bank, (Paper W.P.S, 375).

Datt, R., & Sundharam, K. P. M. (1998): “Indian Economy,” S Chand and Company, New Delhi.

Dev, S. M., and Ravi, C. (2007): “Poverty and Inequality: All India and States 1983-2005,” Economic and Political Weekly, Vol. 42(6), pp. 509-521.

Elisa Wildayana, Imanudin, Junedi, Mohd, Zuhdi, Edi Armanto (2016): “Parameters Affecting Household Income Diversity of Farmer’s Tribes in South Sumatra Tidal Wetland,” Sriwijaya journal of Environment,Vol. 1 No. 3, pp. 47-52.

Friedmann, J. (1960): “Rethinking Poverty: Empowerment and Citizen Rights,” International Social Science Journal, 48(148), pp. 161-172.

Garcia, Y T., Garcia, A. G., M., and Hossain, M. (2000): “Income Distribution and Poverty in Irrigated and Rain fed Ecosystem; The Myanmar Case,” Economic and Political Weekly, Vol. 35(52/53), pp. 4670-4676.

Geetha. K.T. (2011): “Consumption Patterns Among Selected Rural and Urban Households in Coimbatore City,” International Journal of Multidisciplinary Research, vol. 1, issue 2, pp 46-60.

George, S. (1994): "Tribal Development; Legislation Enforcement," New Delhi, 1994, pp.47.

Gopalakrishnan (1993): "A Study of Consumption and Pattern Deviation," Unpublished M.Sc. (Ag.) Thesis submitted to Department of Agricultural Economics, Tamil Nadu Agricultural University, Coimbatore.

Government of Tamil Nadu (2018): Adi Dravidar and Tribal welfare Department, http://www.tn.gov.in/scheme/department_wise/1

Government of Tamil Nadu (2017): "Tamil Nadu Rural Transformation Project (TNRTP)," Report.

Harishankar Banothu (2016): "Tribal Economic Development in India," International Journal of Multidisciplinary Advanced Research Trends Issn: 2349-7408 Volume (III), Issue 1(3), pp.28-34.

Himanshu. (2007): "Recent Trends in Poverty and Inequality: Some Preliminary Results," Economic and Political Weekly, Vol. 42(6), pp. 497-508.

Jayakumar, P. N. (1999): "A Micro Level Study on Poverty and Food Insecurity of Rural Households in Kanchipuram District of Tamil Nadu," Unpublished M.Sc. (Ag.) Thesis submitted to Department of Agricultural Economics, Tamil Nadu Agricultural University, Coimbatore.

Kailasam (1991): "An Econometric Study of Complete Demand System for Rural and Urban Households in Western Tamil Nadu," Unpublished M.Sc. (Ag.) Thesis submitted to Department of Agricultural Economics, Tamil Nadu Agricultural University, Coimbatore.

Karuppaiyan. E, (2,1990): , "Alienation of tribal land in Tamil Nadu," Economic and Political Weekly, Vol-25, No-22, pp-1185-1186

KiranKumar B Dhanappa (2013): "Prevalence of Malocclusion Among Malayali Tribes at Javadu Hills in Polur Taluka, Tamilnadu," Journal of research and advancement in dentistry, pp.38-43. ISSN2278-0076.

Kundu, A., and Sarangi, N. (2007): "Migration, Employment Status and Poverty: An Analysis Across Urban Centers," Economic and Political Weekly, Vol. 42(4), pp. 299-306.

Mahabub Hossain (2004): "Rural Non-Farm Economy, Evidence from Household Survey," Economic and Political Weekly, Vol, XXXIX, No.36, Sep. pp.4053 -4058.

Mahendra Dev et.al (2010): "Food security in India performance, Challenges and polices," Oxfam India working paper series, Oxfam India, New Delhi.

Malya (1961): "An Analysis of Personal Income Distribution in Rural Areas," Indian Journal of Agricultural Economics, 16(1), pp. 187-195.

Manas Das Gupta (1984): "Tribal unrest," Economic and political weekly, Vol. 19, No. 11, PP 449-451.

Meenakshi and Ranjan Ray (2002): "Impact of household size and family composition on poverty in rural India," journal of policy modeling, pp. 539-559.

Ministry of Trible Affairs annual report (2008-09): Government of India, New Delhi Pg. 167.

Ministry of Tribal Affairs (2013): Statistical Profile of Scheduled Tribes in India, Government of India.

M S Meena, K M Singh, R K P Singh, Anjani Kumar, Abhay Kumar and V P Chahal (2017): "Inequality and determinants of income among rural households in tribal dominated areas of Jharkhand," Indian Journal of Agricultural Sciences 87 (1): 92–96.

Nadeem Hasnain (2007): "Tribal India," Palka Prakashan publication, New Delhi. Pg. 378.

Nalini, T. (2010): "An economic assessment of Agricultural and livelihood security among the rural households in Karnataka state," Unpublished M.Sc. (Ag.) Thesis submitted to Department of Agricultural Economics, Tamil Nadu Agricultural University, Coimbatore.

Nandal (1972): "Pattern of Income Investment Expenditure and Savings of Selected Demonstration Farms in Haryana," Indian Journal of Agricultural Economics, 27(4), pp. 11-19.

Narayan Sethi and Hemanta Kumar Phadhan (2012): "The Patterns of Consumption expenditure in Rural Households of Western Odisha of India: An Engel Ratio Analysis," Ontario International development Agency, ISSN: 1923-6654, pp. 117-128.

NCAER (1962): "Long Term Projects of Demand for the Supply of Selected Agricultural Commodities, 1960-61 to 1975-76," National Council of Applied Economic Research, New Delhi.

NCAER. (1989): "Household Income and Its Disposition," National Council of Applied Economic Research, New Delhi.

Ninan. KN (1994): "Poverty and income distributions," Economic and political weekly, pp. 1544-1551.

NSSO (1959): "Note in the Consumer Expenditure Survey," National Sample Survey organization, New Delhi.

NSSO (1989): "Note in the Consumers Expenditure Survey 42nd Round," National Sample Survey organization, New Delhi.

Ojha, P. D. (1970): "A Configuration of Indian Poverty – Inequality and Level of Living Challenges of Poverty in India," Reserve Bank of India Bulletin, 24(1), pp. 16-27.

Padmaja Mishra (1992): "Household consumer expenditure inequalities in India: A decomposition analysis," Review of income and wealth, series 38, no.2, pp.225-236.

Pant, S. P. (1980): "Poverty, Unemployment and Food for Work," Agricultural Situation in India, 35(2), pp. 83-90.

Planning Commission (1992): "Eight Five Year Plan 1992-97," Government of India, New Delhi.

Planning commission reports (2009-10, 2011-12): Government of India, New Delhi.

Prasanna and Kurinjmalar (2017): "Impact of MGNREGP on poverty Alleviation in rural India A Case Study of Two districts in Tamil Nadu," Journal of Academia and Industrial Research (JAIR), Vol.5, Issue 9, Pp. 139-142.

Ponnarasi, T. (2000): "An Economic Analysis of Employment, Income Distribution and Poverty Levels in Varying Irrigation Environs of Coimbatore District," Unpublished M.Sc. (Ag.) Thesis submitted to Department of Agricultural Economics, Tamil Nadu Agricultural University, Coimbatore.

Pradhan and Sethi (2012): "The pattern of consumption expenditure in rural households of Western Odisha of India: An Engel ratio analysis," ODIA international journal of sustainable development, ISSN 1923-6662 (online), available at http:www.ssrn.com/link/ODIA-intl-journal-sustainable-dve. html. pp107-128.

Prabakaran, R. Senthil Kumar,T. and Rao, V.M (2013): "Role of Non-Timber Forest Products in the Livelihood of Malayali Tribe of Chitteri hills of Southern Eastern Ghats, Tamil Nadu, India," Journal of Applied Pharmaceutical science, Vol.3 (05), pp. 056-060.

Pratap (2012): "Livestock for higher, sustainable and inclusive agricultural growth," Economics and political weekly, Vol. XLVII, No. 26-27, pp. 89-98

Pratap and Birthal (2014): "Income sources of farm household in India: Determinates distributional consequences and policy implications," Agricultural Economics Research Review, Vol.27, No.1, pp 37-48.

Prem Nazeer (2015): "Tribals in Tamil Nadu with Special Reference to Tribes of Pachamalai Hills," Historical Research Letter, ISSN 2224-3178 (Paper) ISSN 2225-0964 (Online) Vol 18.

Rajasekhar, Manjula, Suchitra (2017): "Microfinance promote livelihoods and Reduce Vulnerability, Among Adivasis: A study of some NGOs Interventions from Karnataka and Tamil Nadu," Social change, Vol. 47 (1), Sage Publications, Pp. 65-80.

Reddy (1976): "Inter-state differences in social consumption," Economic and political weekly, Vol. 11, No. 24, pp. 872-879.

Thilagavathi, M. (1995): "Impact of Operation Flood on Income and Employment Level in Rural Women – A Study in Madurai District," Unpublished M.Sc. (Ag.) Thesis submitted to Department of Agricultural Economics, Tamil Nadu Agricultural University, Coimbatore.

Sanghamitra Kannongo (2011): "Tribal and Human Rights," Delhi, pp.83-86.

Sathivel (2017): "Role and Contribution of Livestock in Livelihood of Marginal and Landless Livestock Farmers in Rural Tamil Nadu, India," Indian Res. J. Ext. Edu., (Special issue on Veterinary Research & Extension), Pp. 20-25.

Sen, A. K. (1973): "Employment Policy and Technological Choice," Oxford University Press, London.

Sen, A. K. (1976): "Poverty: An Ordinal Approach to Measurement," Econometrica, Vol. 44(2), pp. 219-231.

Sen, A. (1999): "Development as Freedom," Anchor Books Publishing Company, New York.

Sidhu (1974): "On the Economic Inequality Statistics Canada," Oxford: Clarendum press, pp. 205-210.

Singh, K.S (2006): "The Scheduled Tribe," Vol. III, Chennai, pp.736.

Sethia Savneet. (2013): "India's Changing Consumption Pattern," *Gyanpratha-Accman Journal of Management*, volume 5, issue 2.

Sivasakthidevi (2010): "Rural Employment Generation Programmes Vs Food Subsidy Programmes- An Economic Analysis of Household Employment, Consumption and Welfare in Tamil Nadu," Unpublished M.Sc. (Ag.) Thesis submitted to Department of Agricultural Economics, Tamil Nadu Agricultural University, Coimbatore.

Sivakumar (1976): "Family size consumption expenditure, income, and land holding on agrarian economy: A Critique of some populist nation," Economic and Political Weekly, Vol. 11, No,30, pp.1115+1117-1124.

Soundarpadian and Yamuna (2017): "Role of Non-Timber Forest Products in Poverty Reduction Among Tribals in Western Ghats of Tamil Nadu," Asian Journal for Poverty Studies, Vol. 3 (2), Pp. 53-58.

Sundar, A. (2012): "Impact of Mahathma Gandhi National Rural Employment Guarantee Programme (MGNREGs) On Rural Households of Sivagangai Distrct of Tamil Nadu: An Economic Analysis," Unpublished Ph.D Thesis submitted to Department of Agricultural Economics, Tamil Nadu Agricultural University, Coimbatore.

Sundara Rao (2012): "Determinants Of Poverty In Tribal Households In Andhra Pradesh (A Study On Visakhapatnam District," International Journal Of Multidisciplinary Educational Research, ISSN: 2277-7881, Volume 1, Issue 2, pp-38-46.

Sundram (2003): "Poverty among social and economic groups in India in 1990," Economic and political weekly, Vol. 38, No. 50, pp. 5263-5276

Sunitha A. (2007): "An Economic Analysis of Urban Food Consumption in Coimbatore city," Unpublished M.Sc. (Ag.) Thesis submitted to Department of Agricultural Economics, Tamil Nadu Agricultural University, Coimbatore

Swarnam, Velmurugan and Saravana Kumar (2015): " Studies on Tribal Farming in Nicobar Islands, India," IOSR Journal of Agriculture and Veterinary Science (IOSR-JAVS), Volume 8, Issue 1 Ver. II (Jan. 2015), PP 41-49.

Swenson & Jureen (1953): "Demand Analysis: A Study in Econometrics," John Willey and Sons Publications, New York.

United Nations. (1995): "Report of the World Summit for Social Development," accessed from http://www.un.org/esa/socdev/docs/summit.pdf.

United Nations (2013): "State of the World's Indigenous Peoples."

Vaidialingam (1980): "A Study on Employment, Income and Expenditure pattern of Landless Labour and Rural Artisans," Unpublished M.Sc. (Ag.) Thesis submitted to Department of Agricultural Economics, Tamil Nadu Agricultural University Coimbatore.

Vedeld, Angelsen, Bojo (2007): "Forest Environmental Income and the Rural Poor," Forest Policy and Economics, Vol. 9 (7), Pp. 869-879.

Venkatram (2003): "Assessment of food Security in Rural households – A study in Southern Tamil Nadu," Unpublished M.Sc. (Ag.) Thesis submitted to Department of Agricultural Economics, Tamil Nadu Agricultural University, Coimbatore.

Vidyarthi, L.P. and Rai, B.K. (1960): "The Tribal Culture of India," Delhi, pp.412.

Vijay Nayak and Shalaja Prasad (1984): "On Level of Living of Scheduled Castes and Scheduled Tribes," Economic and Political Weekly, Vol. 19, No. 30, pp.1205-1213.

Willard & Bell (1956): "The Economics of Consumption and Economics of Decision Mainly in the Households," McGraw Hill Book Company, New York.

World Bank (2007): "Jharkhand: Addressing the Challenges of Inclusive Development," Report No. 36437-IN Poverty Reduction and Economic Management. India Country Management Unit, South.

World Bank (2016): "Poverty and Shared Prosperity Taking on Inequality," Libratory of Congress Cataloging In-publication data has been applied, ISBN- 978-1-4648-0958-3.

Yashwant (1963): "Income and Levels in Some South India Villages," Indian Journal of Agricultural Economics, 18(1), pp. 302.

Zalak Shah (2013): "The Income and Expenditure Pattern of Families at the Bottom of the Pyramid," Unpublished research work, accessed by Google scholar.

Websites:

http://www.tn.gov.in/scheme. Accessed data 25-09-2017.

http://asiancenturyinstitute.com/society/804-asia-s-indigenous-peoplesAccessed 12-09-2017.

Maps

Map 1: India and Tamil Nadu.

Map 2: Thiruvannamalai District.

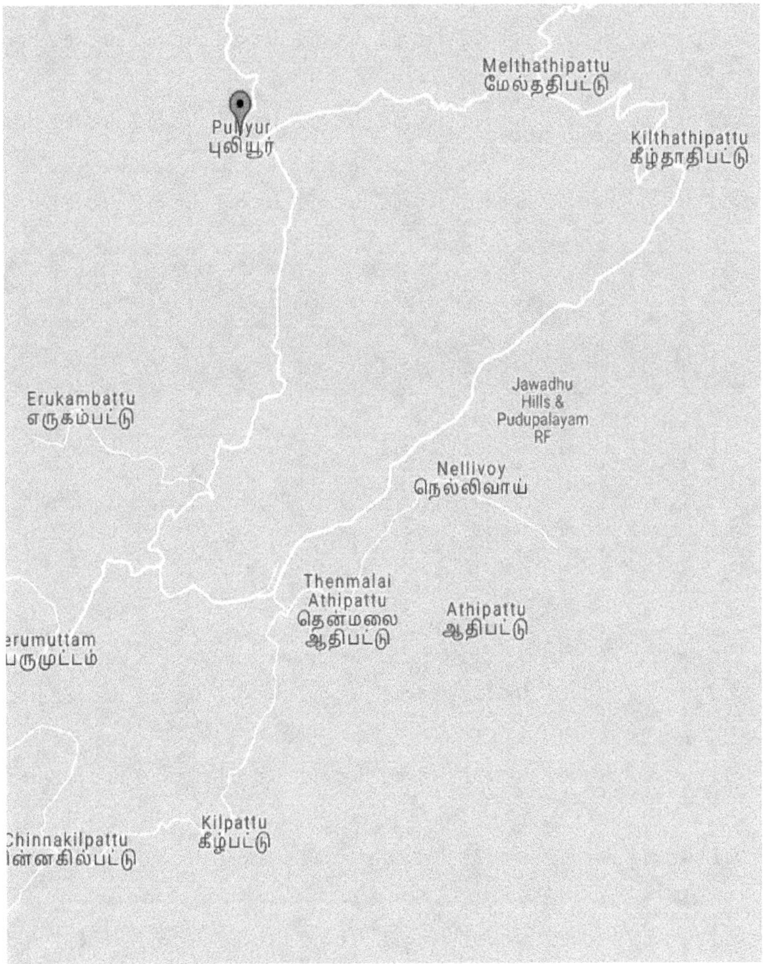

Map 3: Puliyur Village Panchyath.

Study Area Photographs

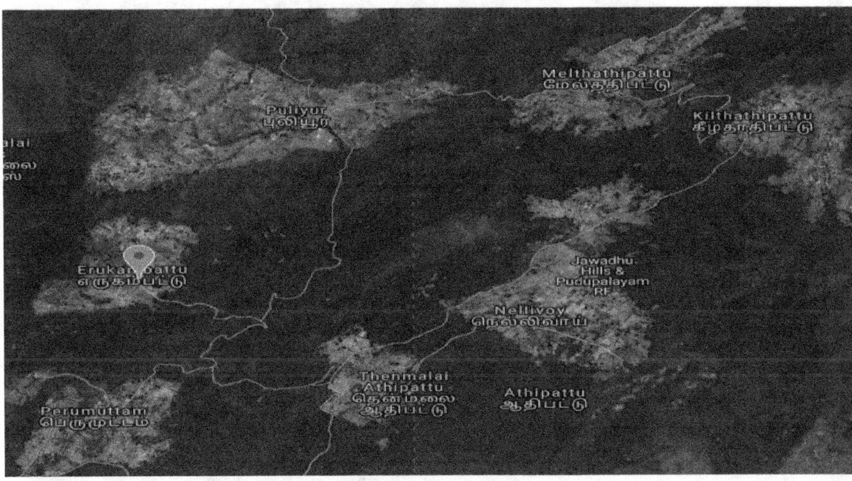

Photo 1. Puliyur Panchayath Hamlets.

Photo 2. Cultivation land and Road.

Photo 3. Cultivation land.

Photo 4. Weekly Market in Jamunamathur.

Photo 5. Weekly Market in Jamunamathur.

Photo 6. MGNREGP Work.

Photo 7. Puliyru Village Hamlet Road.

Photo 8 Puliyru Village Hamlet Road.

Photo 9 Puliyru Village Hamlet Road.

Charts

Chart: 1 Total income of the respondent households

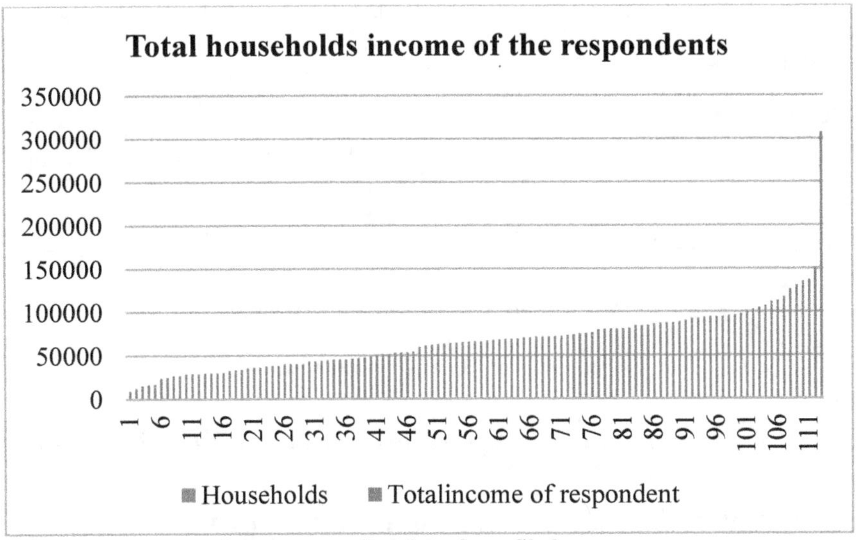

Source: compiled data from filed survey.

Chart: 2 Total expenditure on food and non-food items

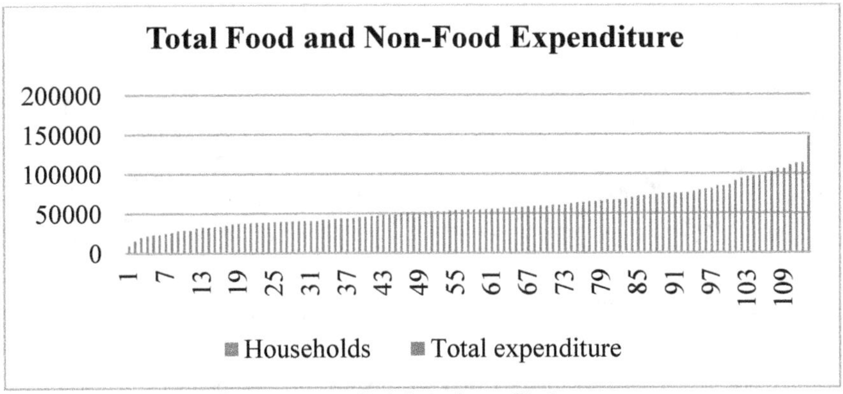

Source: compiled data from filed survey

Note: Line denotes that mean value of expenditure.

Chart: 3 Per capita income of the respondent households

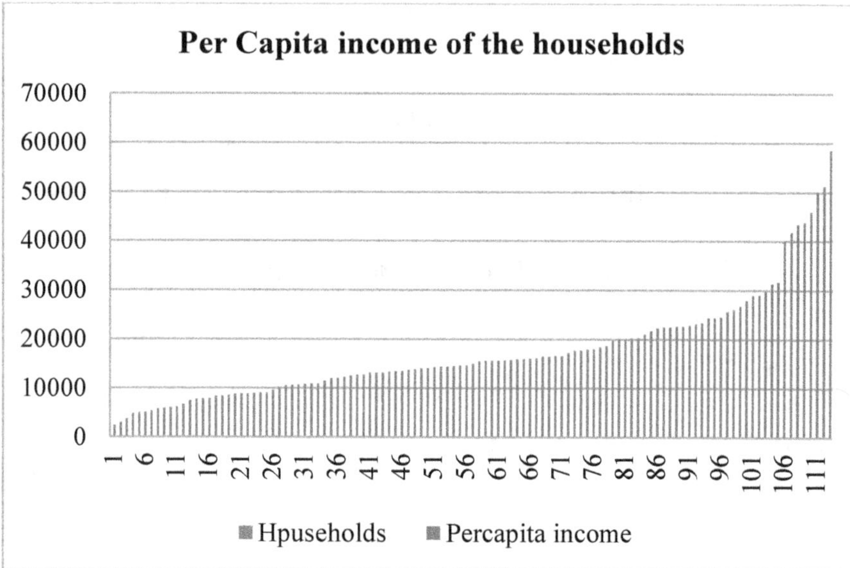

Source: compiled data from filed survey.

Chart: 4 Per capita total expenditure of respondent households

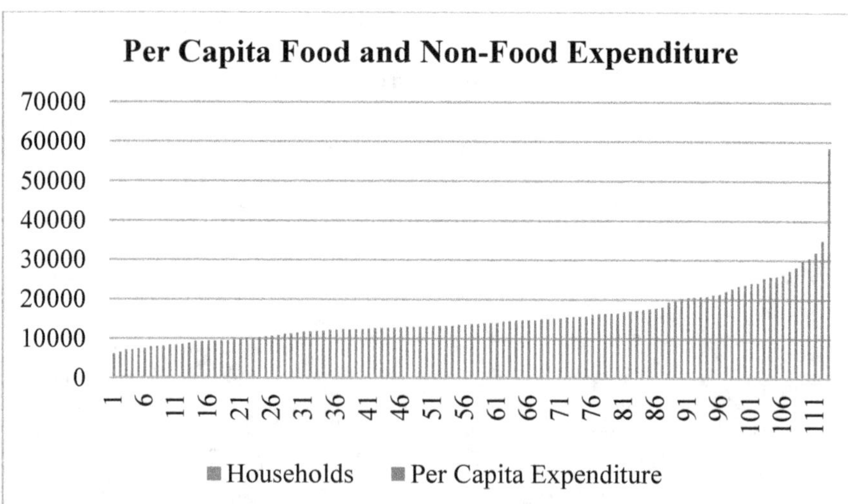

Source: compiled data from filed survey

Note: Line denotes that mean value of the income.

Major indigenous groups in South Asian sub-region countries

Country	Commonly referred names	Major indigenous groups	Approximate population
Bangladesh	Tribal, upajati, indigenous hill tribe, Jumna, indigenous hill men, aboriginal tribes	Bawm, Chak, Chakma, Khumi, Khyang, Lushai, Marma, Mro, Pangkhua, Tanchangya Tripura and others collectively known as Jumma and Adivasi in plain, including Santal, Banais, Bhuiyas, Bhumijies, Dalus, Garos, Gonds, Hadis, Hajangs, Hos, Kharias, Kharwars, Kochs, Koras, Maghs (Bakarganj District), Mal Paharias, Oraons, Maches, Mundas, Santhals, Sauria Paharias, Turis and others	1.7-3.7 million (1.2-2.5 per cent)
Bhutan		Sarchops, Khengs, Adivasi, Birmi, Brokpa, Doya, Lepcha, Toktop and others	Approximately 10 per cent of the total popu-lation
India	Scheduled Tribes or Adivasi (original inhabitants);	461 groups recognized; major groups include Gond, Oraon, Khond, Bhil, Mina, Onge, Jarawa, Nagas and others	84.3 million, they comprise 8.2 per cent of the total population
Nepal	Indigenous Nationalities (Adivasi Janajati)	Magar, Tharu, Tamang, Newar, Rai, Gurung, Limbu and others	8.4 million people, or 37.19 per cent of the total population
Pakistan		Pashtun, Sindhis, Baluchs, Kihals and Mors, Buzdar, Kailasha and others	Not available
Sri Lanka		Vyadha ("huntsmen/archers") or Vadda	1,229 and 4,510 people,

Source: State of the World's Indigenous Peoples (United Nations) 201.

World and Regional Poverty Estimation, 2013.

Si. No	Region	Headcount Ratio (%)
1	East Asia and Pacific	3.5
2	Eastern Europe and Central Asia	2.3
3	Latin America and the Caribbean	5.4
4	Middle East and North Africa*	NA
5	South Asia	15.1
6	Sub-Saharan Africa	41.0
	Total (six regions)	12.6
	World	10.7

***Sources:* Annex 2A; most recent estimates, based on 2013 data using Povcal Net (online analysis tool), World Bank, Washington, DC, http://iresearch.worldbank.org/PovcalNet/.Note: Poverty is measured using the 2011 US$1.90-a-day PPP poverty line. The six-region total includes all developing regions. World includes all developing regions, plus industrialized countries. Definitions of geographical regions are those of PovcalNet.**

***Data is not available**

A Study on Household Income and Expenditure Patterns of Scheduled Tribes in Tamil Nadu

Part I: General information

1. Name of Village:___________ Block:_____________ District_________________
2. Name of respondent or head of the household: ______________________
3. Community of the respondent:___________________________
4. Type of family: 0=Joint family, 1=Nuclear family, 2=Separate.
5. Household demographic characteristics

S. No	Family Members	Relation	Age	Sex	Education	Main Occupation	Secondary Occupation
1							
2							
3							
4							
5							
6							
7							
8							
9							
10							

Part II: Basic amenities of household

5. Do you have own house? (No / Yes). If yes, what type of house? _____________, present value of the house (in Rs________). If rent, present rent per month (in Rs__________)

6. Do you have house ownership certificate (Patta) (No / Yes).

7. Do you have Ration card (No / Yes).

8. Do you have drinking water connection in your home (No / Yes). If yes, is it potable? (No / Yes). . If you do not have drinking water connection, where do you access the water, distance from your home (in Km)? _____________

9. Do you have toilet facility in your home (No / Yes). If yes, are you use. If no, which one do you use? _______________

10. Do you have electrical connection in your house (No / Yes). If yes / No, what was the sources? _______________

10. Household items.

Si. no	Household Items	Number	Present Value	Where purchased	
				market	Govt.
1	Radio				
2	Television				
3	Mixer grinder				
4	Grinder				
5	Fan				
6	Table fan				
7	LPG stove				
8	Kerosene stove				
9	Refrigerator				
10	Washing machine				
11	Computer				
12	Laptop				
13	Emergence lamp				
14	Inviter				
15	Mobile phone				
16	Telephone				
17	Bicycle				
18	Motorbike				
19	Car				
20	Others				

Part III

3.1 Income from the land

11. Do you have agricultural land?

S. No	Type of Land	*Leased in	*Leased out	Total Acres	Present value of the land
1	Dry land				
2	Wet land				

***Note: Leased-in, leased out, what methods they followed?**

12. Crop wise income.

S. No	Crop wise	Acre	Total quantity	Total value bag(in Rs)	Marketed by Govt. / Pvt.	Total cost
1						
2						
3						
4						

13. Agricultural wage present and last 5 years back? Male:____/_____, female:____/_____.

14. Where did you get the agricultural seeds (Govt. / Pvt.)? That seeds are hybrid?

15. Where did you get agricultural inputs (Govt. / Pvt.)? That inputs are organic or inorganic?

16. What kind of the irrigation sources do you use to your agricultural land?

17. Do you own agricultural equipment?

Si. No	Items	Quantity	Present Value	Working / not-working	maintenance cost
1	Tractor / Trailer				
2	Sprayer power/ hand				
3	Weeder				
4	Pump set (oil / power/ solar)				
5	Hand driller				
6	Bullock cart				
7	Cattle shed				
8	Others				
	Total				

3.2 Livestock income

18. Do you have livestock in your family?

Si. No	Livestock	Numbers	Present Values	Milk* income	Number sold In the last one year	Amount Receive	Average of maintenance cost
1	Cow and calf						
2	Bull						
3	Buffalo and calf						
4	Goat and kid						
5	Sheep and lamb						
6	Hen and chicken						
7	Others						

* where do they selling?________________________________

3.3 Forest based income

19. Non-Forest based produce collated.

Si. No	Name of produce	No. of month	Unit	Average prices per Unit	Total value
1					
2					
3					
4					
5					
6					
	Total				

Code: 1.Tamarind, 2.Nellikai, 3.Yettikottai, 4.Avaram Bark, 5.Konnai Bark, 6.Kadukkai,7.Pungan, 8.Tagarai, 9.Manipungan, 10.Seekai, 11.Woodapple, 12.Elandai, 13.Kilakkai, 14.Setha, 15.Goa

3.4 Secondary Income sources

20. Household Income from other sources.

Si. No	Name of the work	Male	Female	No. of Month	Average per day	Total
1	Industrial labour work					
2	Construction work					
3	Wood cutting work					
4	MGNREGP					
5	Migration labour					

21. Financial assistances from Government schemes (last one year)

Si. No	Name of the scheme	Number of persons	Total amount
1	Old Age pension		
2	Government scheme for Marriage fund		
3	Dr. Muthulakshmi Reddy maternity benefit scheme		
4	Scholarships from school / colleges		
5	compensation for natural hazards		
6	Government livelihood assistances (cattle)		
7	Others		

Part IV

4.1 Consumption Expenditure

22. Household food and Non-food expenditure.

Si. No	Item	Village (1)/ Town(2)	Quantity (Kgs)	Unit value (Rs)	Total consumer expenditure per month		
					Own	Purchased	Govt.
I	**I Food items per month**						
1	Rice						
2	Wheat						
3	Pulse						
4	Edible oil						
5	Vegetables						
6	Green Vegetables						
7	Black-gram						
8	Red-gram						
9	Milk						

	II Millets products					
10	Ragi					
11	Samai					
12	Kampu					
13	Maize					
14	Horse-gram					
15	Other Millet					
	IV Spices product					
16	Chilly powder					
17	Salt					
18	Turmeric powder					
19	Sugar					
20	Tamarind					
21	Black pepper, cumin seed, Aniseed.					
22	Ginger (dry) chilly, Asafetida,					
23	Other spices					
	III Meat items					
24	Mutton					
25	Chicken					
26	Egg					
27	Beef					
28	Fish					
29	Pork					
30	Others					
	V Drinks and others					
31	Tobacco leaf					
32	Tobacco product					
33	Liquor					
34	Others					
	VI Ready to eat food					
35	Snacks					
36	Sweets					
37	Cooked food					
38	Fruits and nuts					
	Non – Food items 365 days					

	VI Cooking items						
39	Fire wood (p.m.)*						
40	Kerosene(p.m.)*						
41	LPG(p.m.)*						
	VII Cloths and cosmetics						
42	Cloths						
43	Foot wears						
44	Washing bar (p.m.)*						
45	Bathing bar (p.m.)*						
46	Bag						
47	Cosmetics (p.m.)*						
	VIII Bills and payments						
48	Electrical bill (p.m.)*						
49	Petrol cost (p.m.)*						
50	Cable TV bills (p.m.)*						
51	Entertainment (p.m.)*						
52	Mobil recharge (p.m.)*						
53	Trances port cost (p.m.)*						
54	Hair catting						
55	Furnishers items						
56	Kitchen appliances						
57	Jewelers						
58	Others						
	Grand total non-food expenditure						
	Grand total food expenditure						
	All total						

***Note: (p.a.) per month.**

4.2 Educational Expenditure

23. Does anyone of your children study at school / colleges?

S. No	Name	Village/ Town	Standard	Institution	Books & note books expenditure (p.a)	Transport cost per month	Annual fee
1							
2							
3							
4							
Total cost							
	Grand total						

4.3 Health expenditure

24. Did you family have any medical expenditure in last one month.

Si. No	Number of persons	Village / Town	Type of hospital Govt./Pvt.	Hospital & medical Cost lost month	Transport cost lost month	Other cost last month specify
1						
2						
3						
4						
	Total expenditure					

Part V- 5.1 Banking & Savings

25. Did your family members have saving account in the financial institutions?

Si. No	Post Office Account 0=No/ 1=Yes	If yes, how much amount do you have now	Do you have Bank Account? 0=No/ 1=Yes	If yes, how much amount do you have now	Are you SHG member? 0=No/ 1=Yes	If yes, how much amount do you save?	How much money you borrowed from SHG in the last one year?	Did you purchase any bonds from bank/ post office? If yes, how much?	Did you get any credit from financial institutions? If yes, how much?
1									
2									
3									
4									
5									

26. Did you borrow money from Pvt. Finical institution Yes / No. if Yes give the details and what was the interest rate?

www.ingramcontent.com/pod-product-compliance
Lightning Source LLC
LaVergne TN
LVHW010719210926
848485LV00008B/1454/J